MAKE POINT ONE VOLUME TWO

MAP BOOK PUBLISHERS

Point One
Volume Two

Editor : MP Ko
Photographer : Chang Hatla, Anothermountainman, Shu Lai
Graphic Design : Anothermountainman

First published 2005 by
MAP BOOK PUBLISHERS
5th Floor, 231 Wing Lok Street
Sheung Wan, Hong Kong
Tel: (852) 2546 3016
mapoff@navigator.com

Available in North, South and Central America through
D.A.P./Distributed Art Publishers Inc
155 Sixth Avenue, 2nd Floor, N.Y 10013
tel (212) 627 1999   Fax (212) 627 9484

Available in Europe through
IDEA BOOKS
Nieuwe Herengracht 11, 1011 RK Amsterdam, NL.
tel +31 20 6226154   Fax +31 20 6209299

Available in Hong Kong through
MAP BOOK PUBLISHERS
3/F 231 Wing Lok Street
Sheung Wan, Hong Kong
Tel (852) 2546 3016

ISBN 988-98395-6-2

Printed in China, 2005
www.map-office.com

Point One
Volume Two

Editor : Ma Ke
Photographer : Zhang Hai'er, Anothermountainman, Shu Lei
Graphic Design : Anothermountainman

First published 2005 by
MAP BOOK PUBLISHERS
5th Floor, 231, Wing Lok Street
Sheung Wan, Hong Kong
Tel: (852) 2546 3016
mapoff@netvigator.com

Available in North, South and Central America through
D.A.P. / Distributed Art Publishers Inc
155 Sixth Avenue, 2nd Floor, N.Y.10013
Tel: (212) 627–1999   Fax: (212) 627–9484

Available in Europe through
IDEA BOOKS
Nieuwe Herengracht 11, 1011 RK Amsterdam, NL
Tel: +31 20 6226154   Fax: +31 20 6209299

Available in Hong Kong through
MAP BOOK PUBLISHERS
5/F, 231 Wing Lok Street
Sheung Wan, Hong Kong
Tel: (852) 2546 3016

ISBN 988-98395-6-3

Printed in China, 2005
www.map-office.com

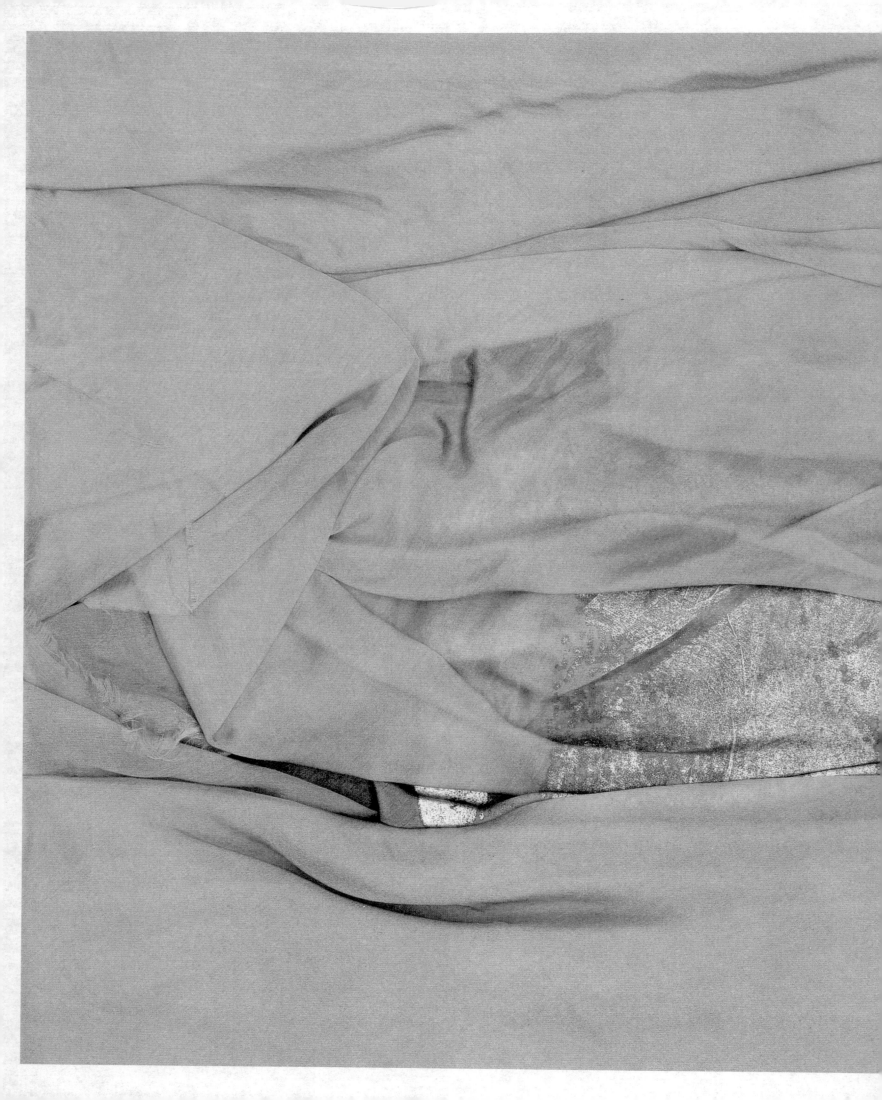

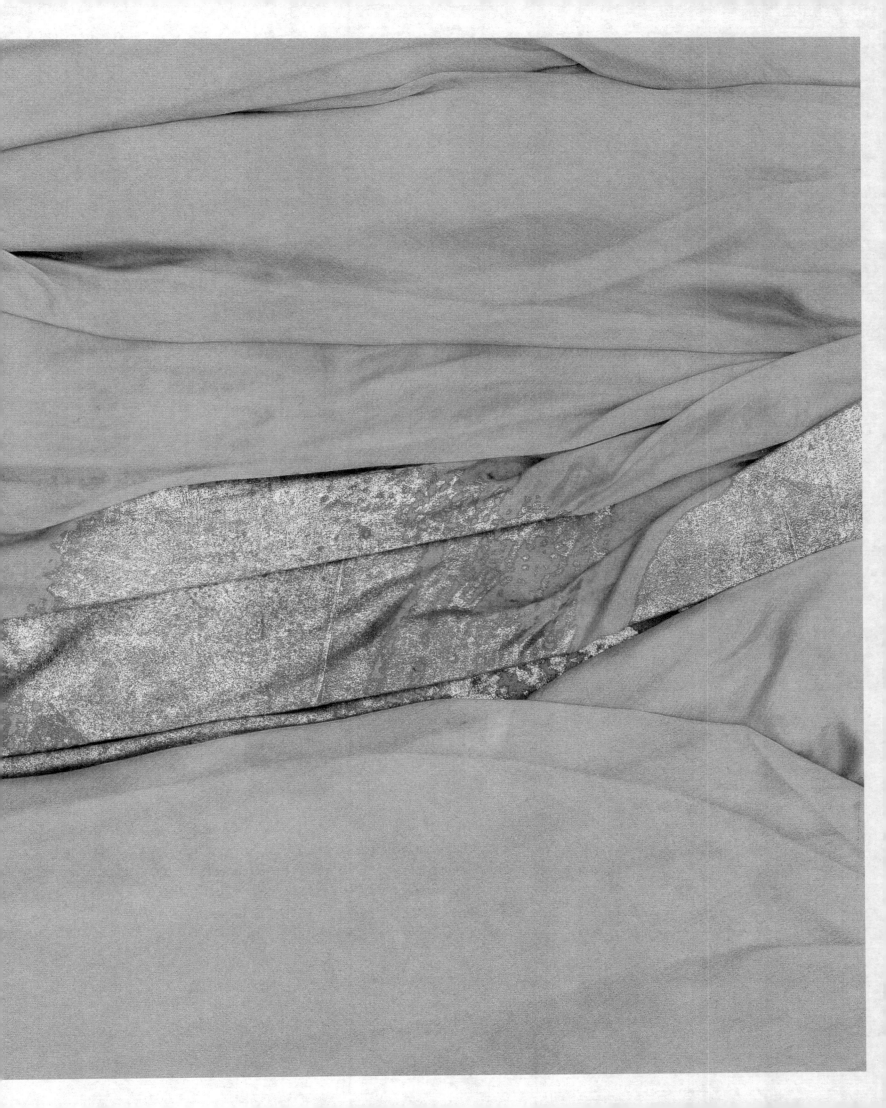

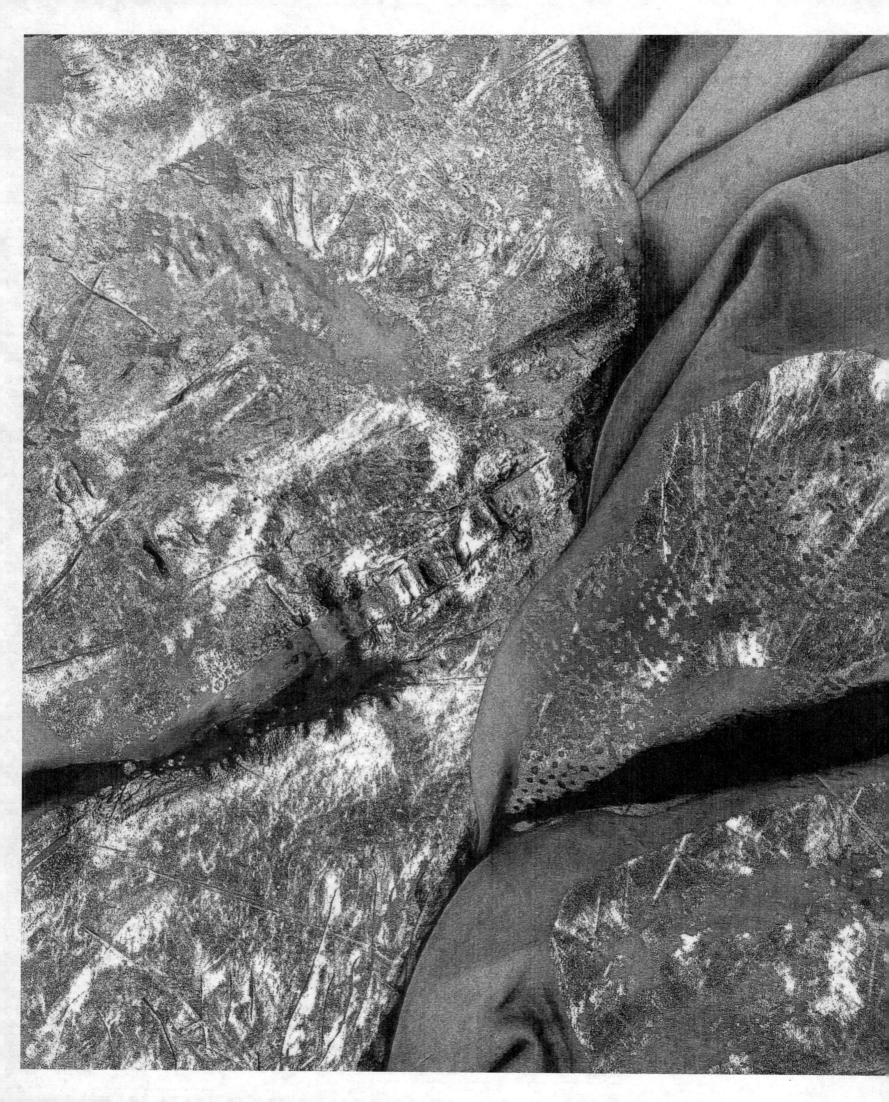

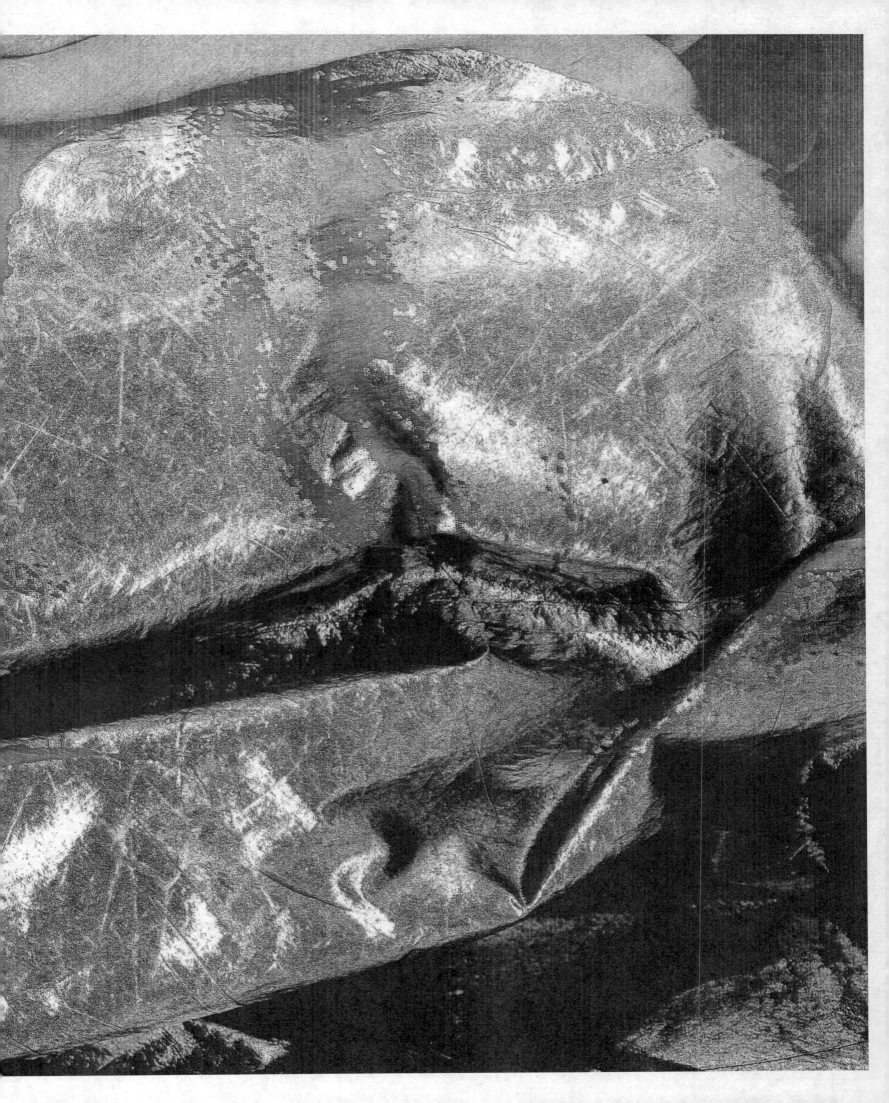

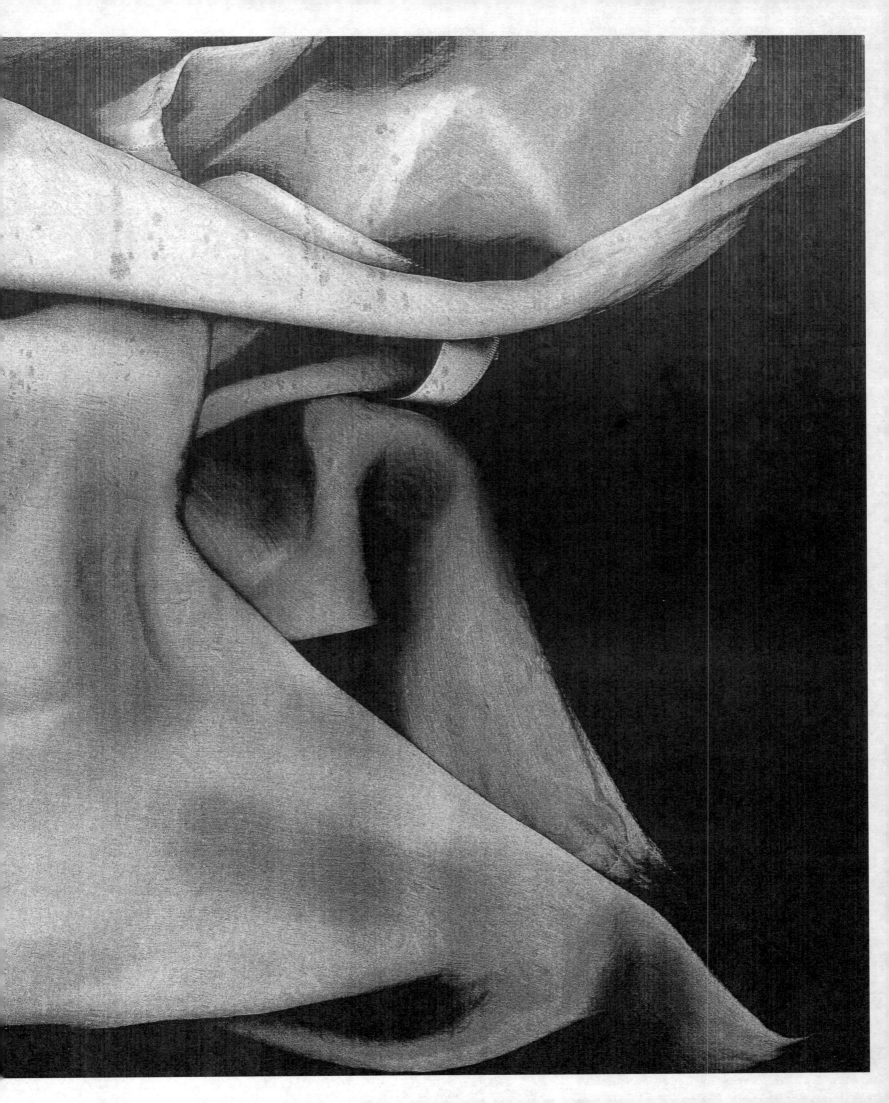

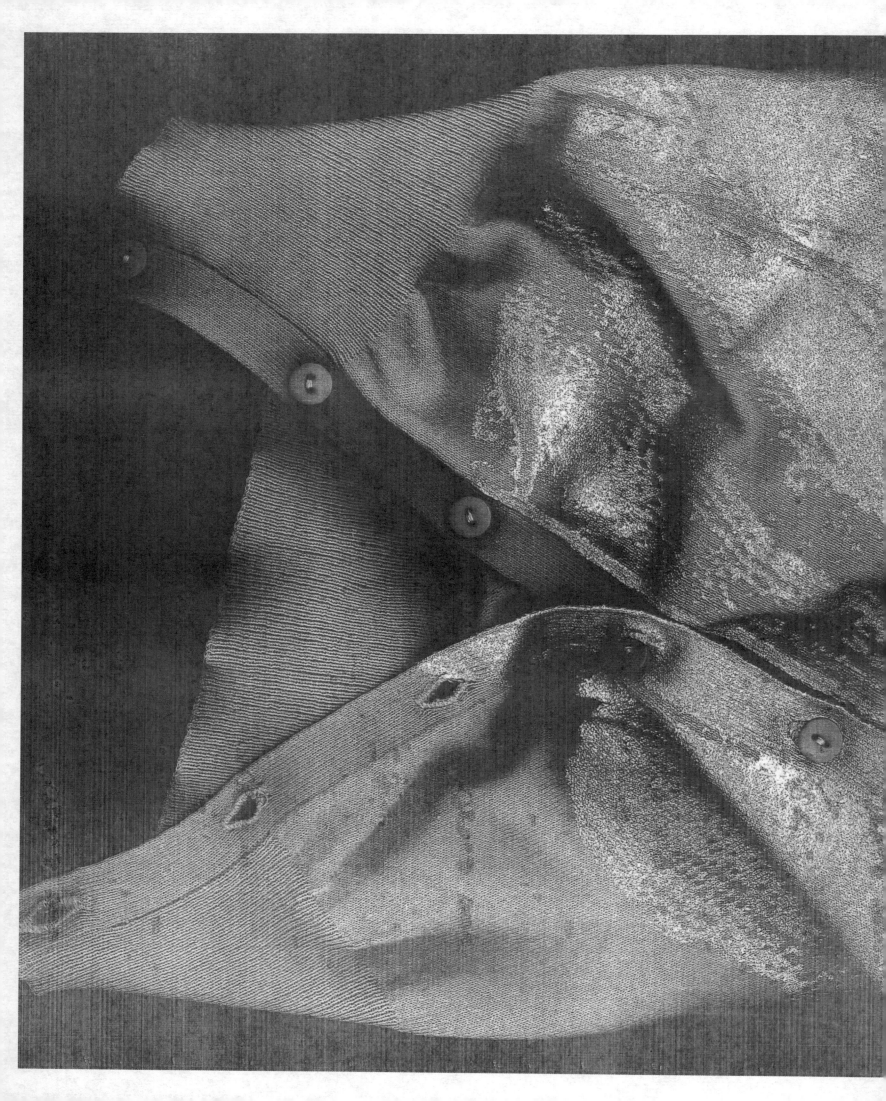

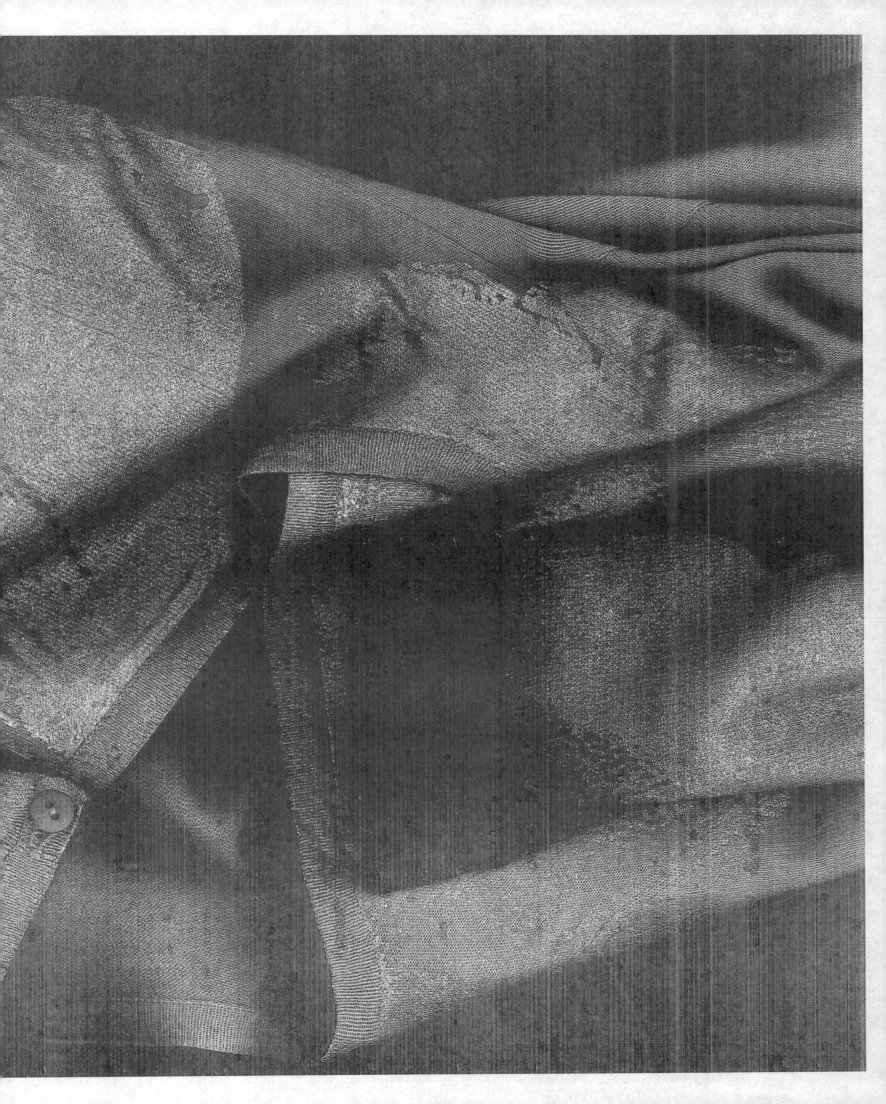

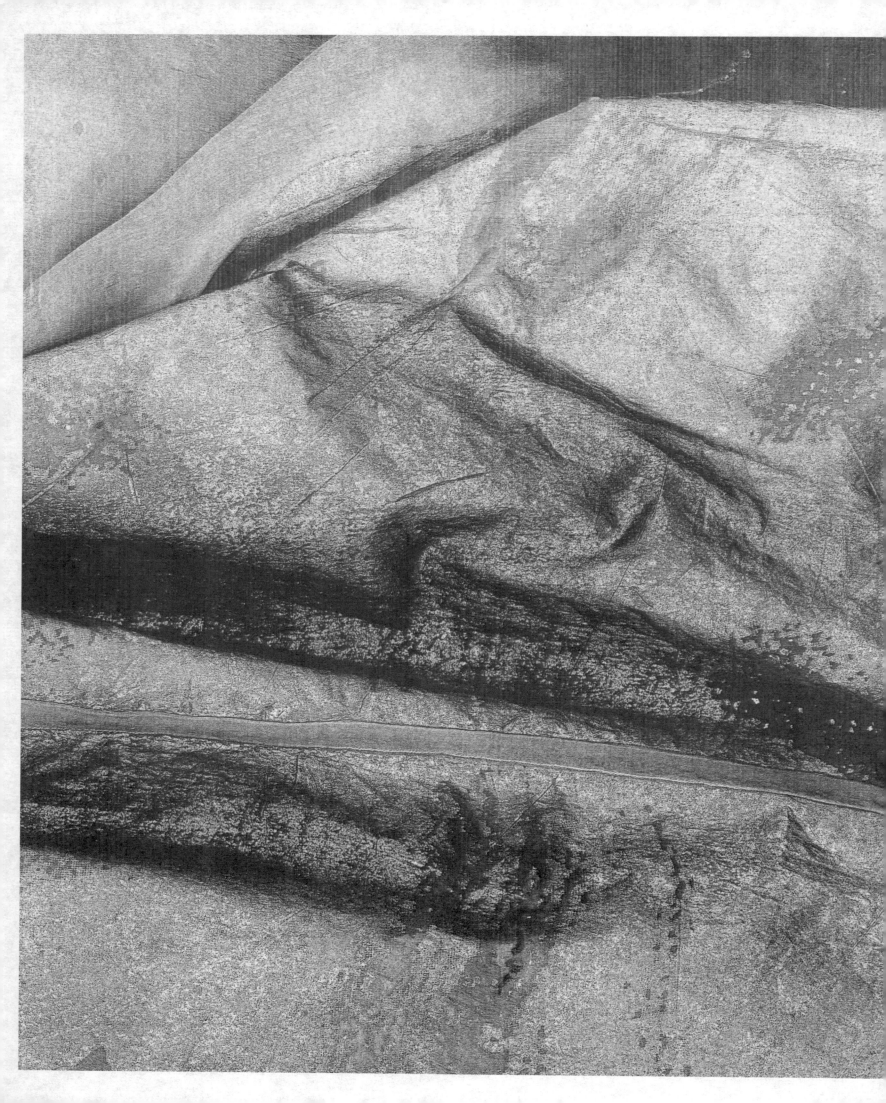

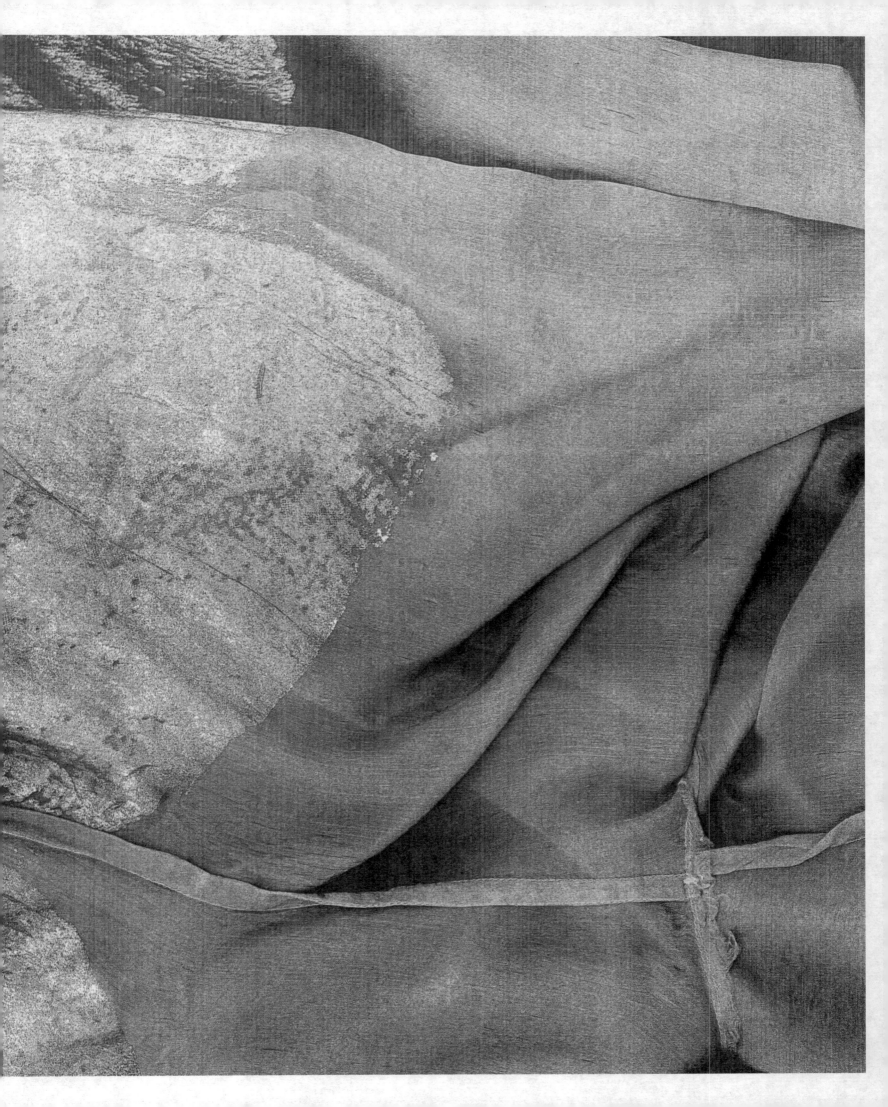

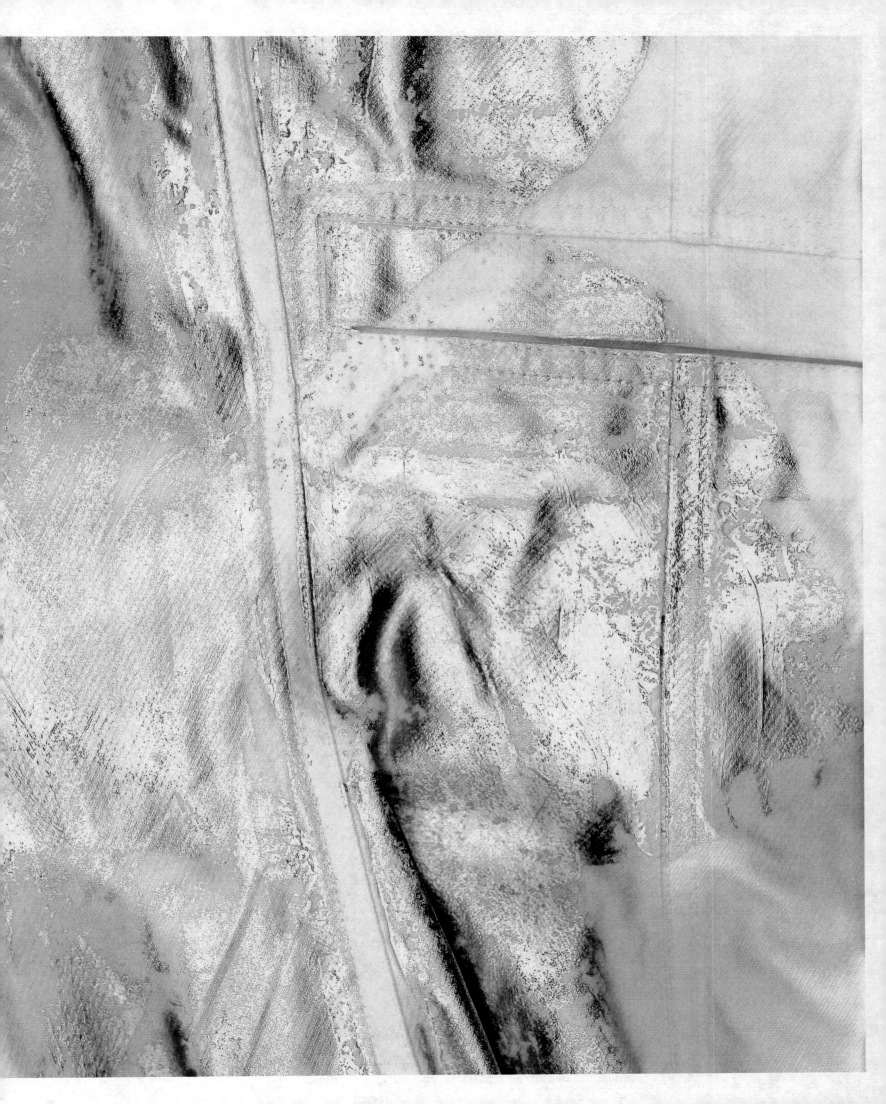

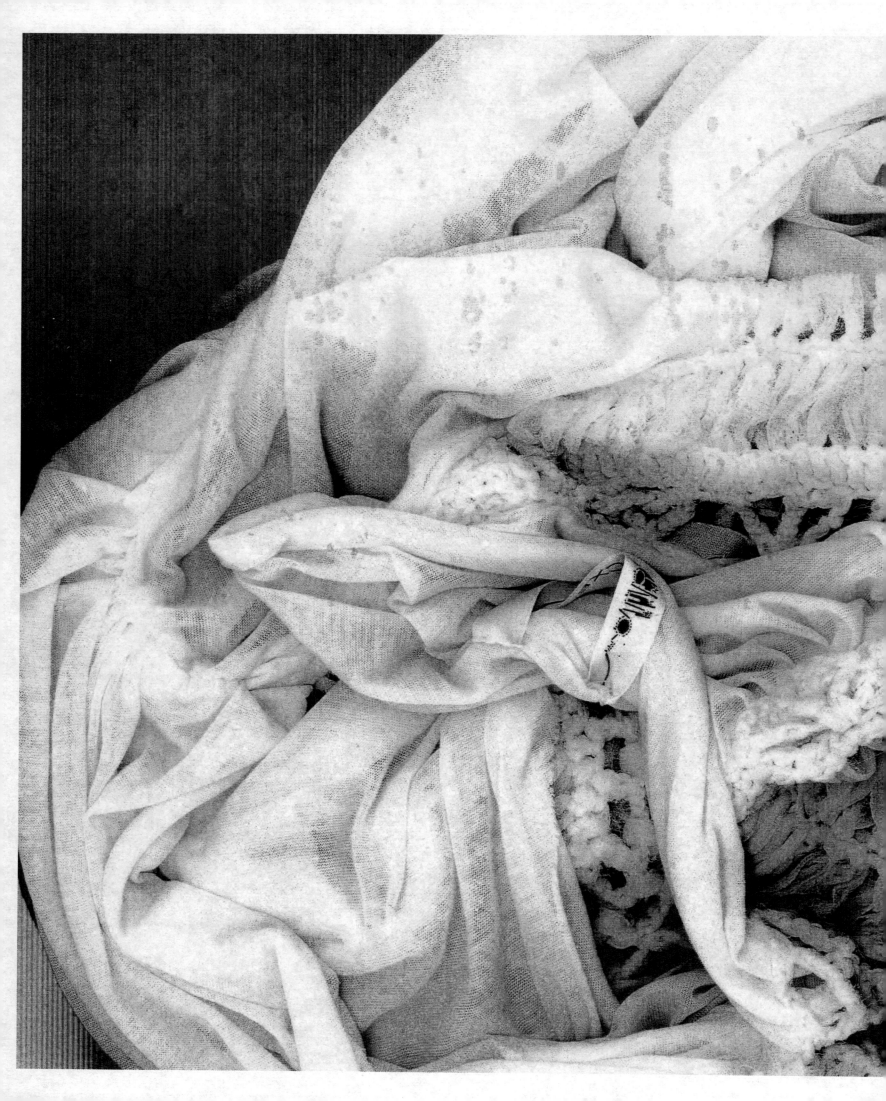

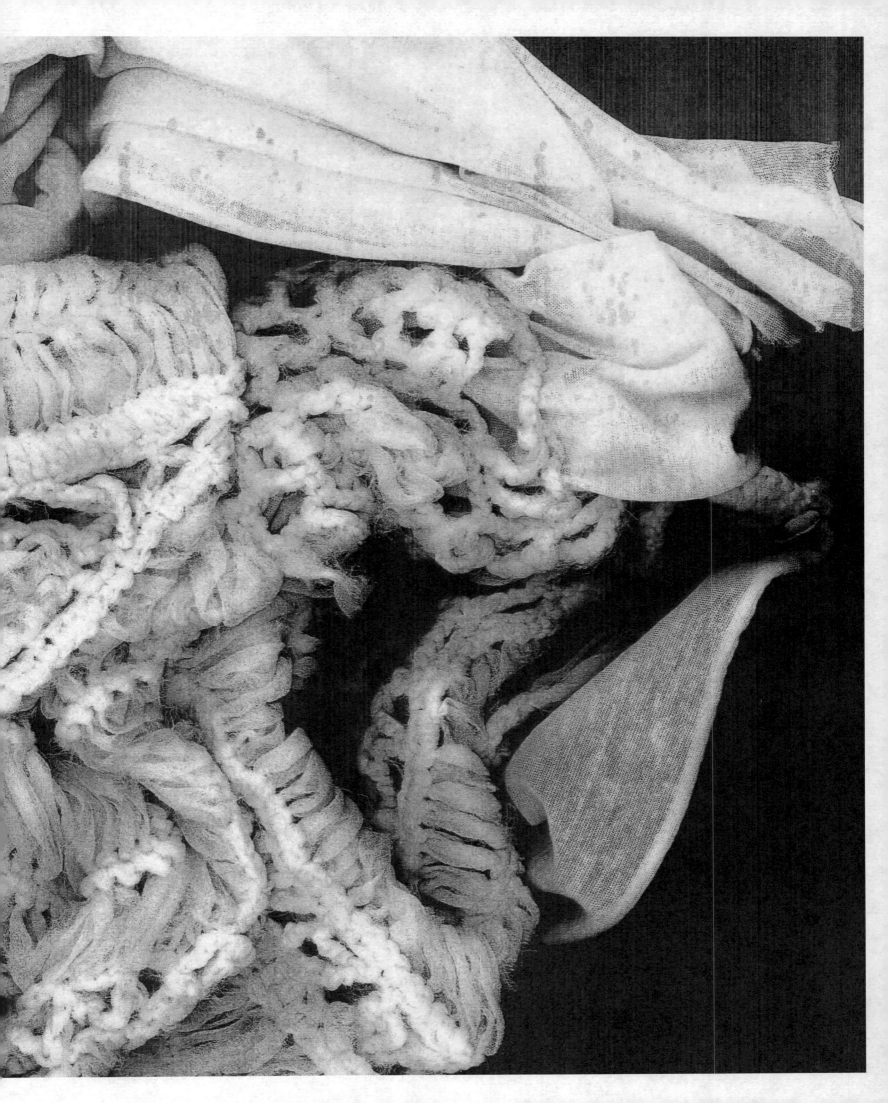

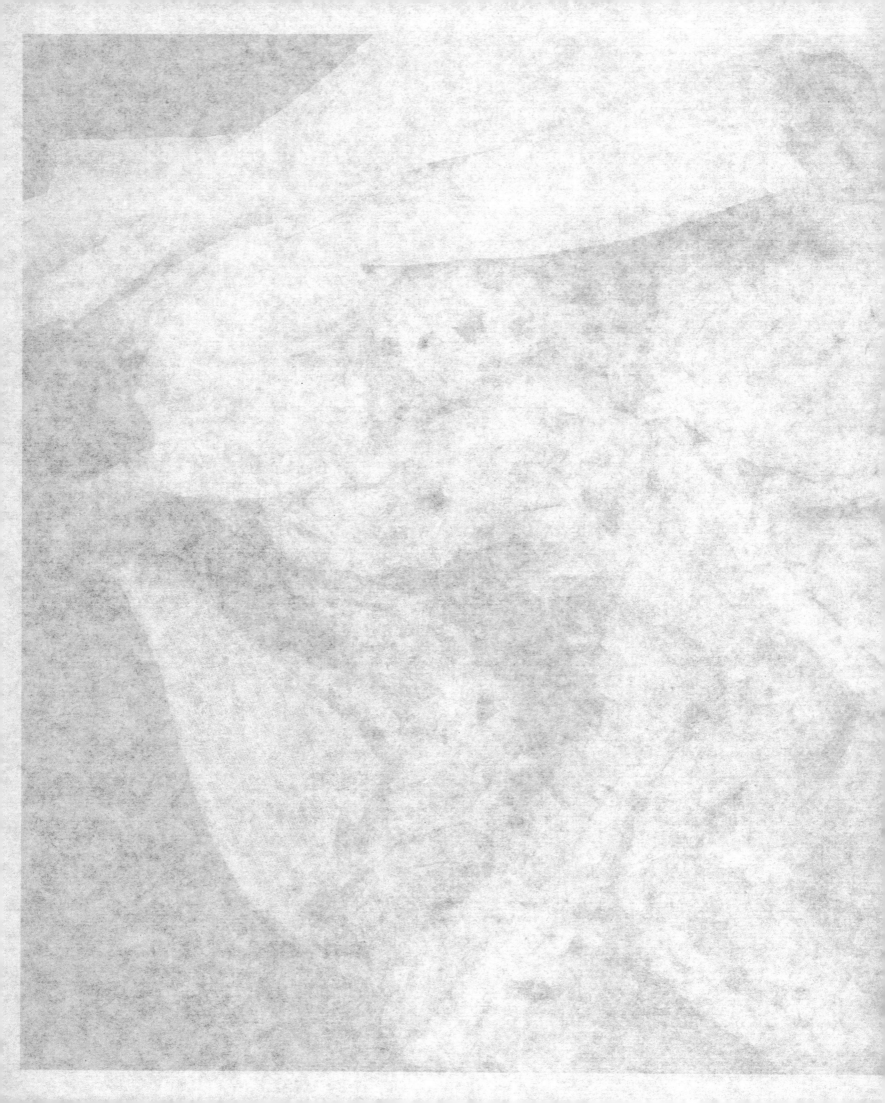

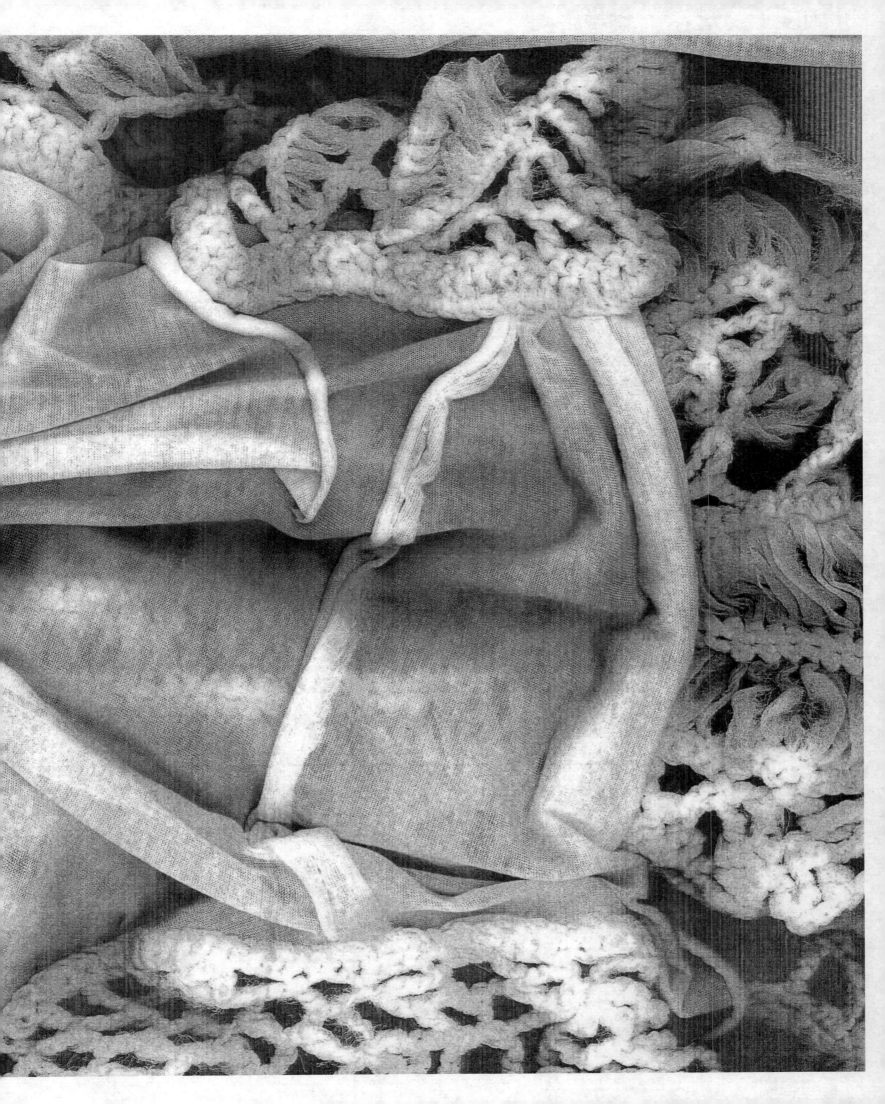

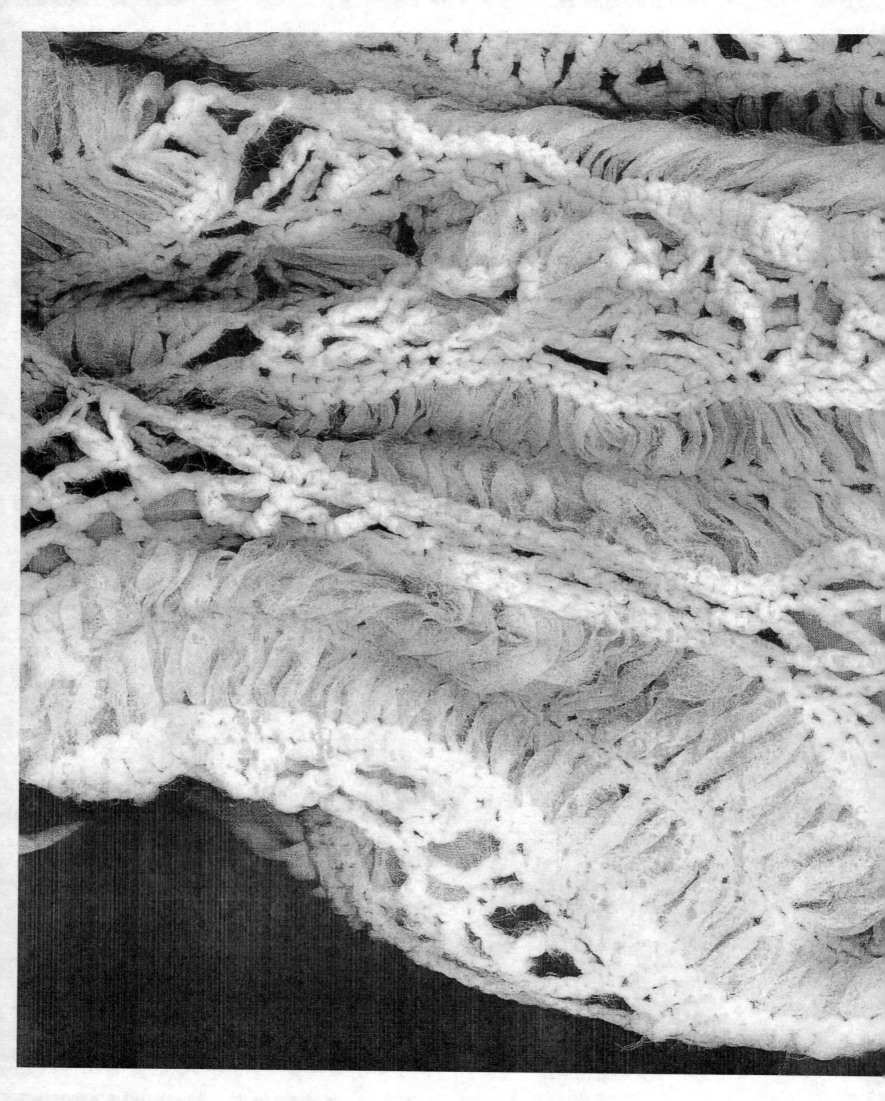

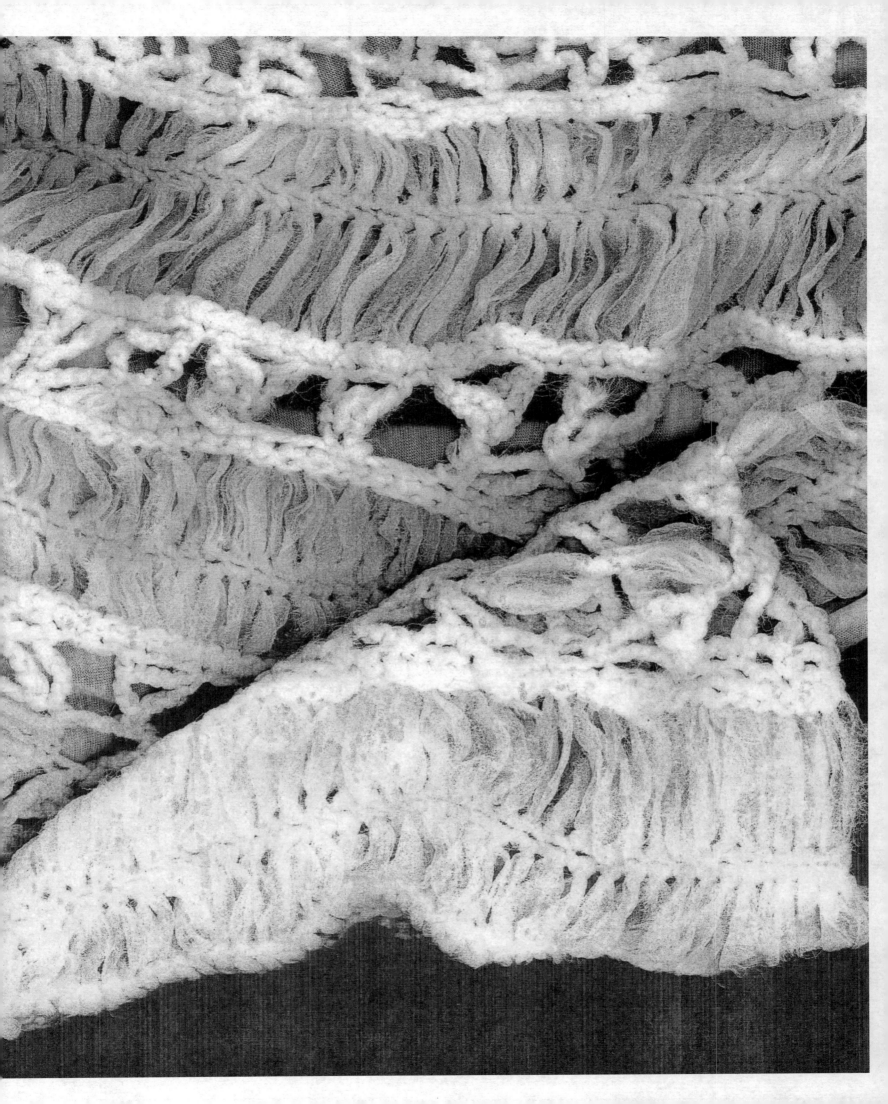

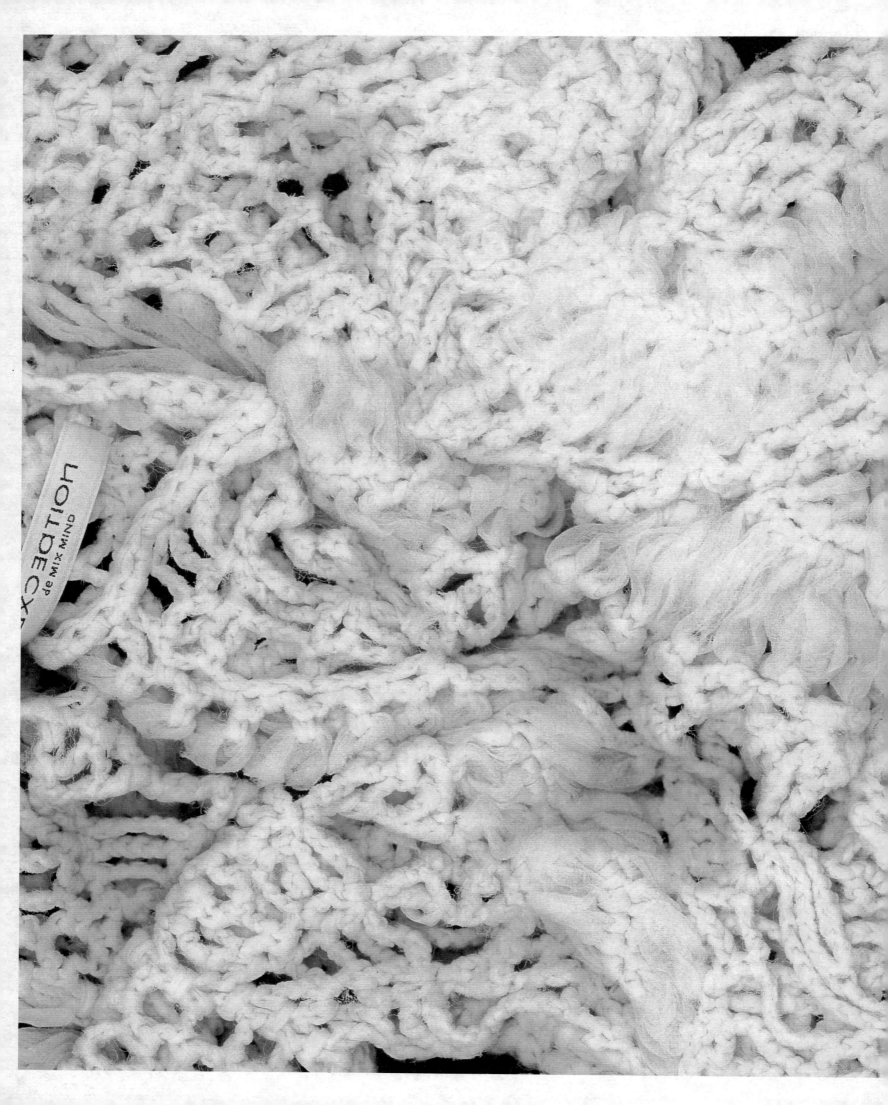

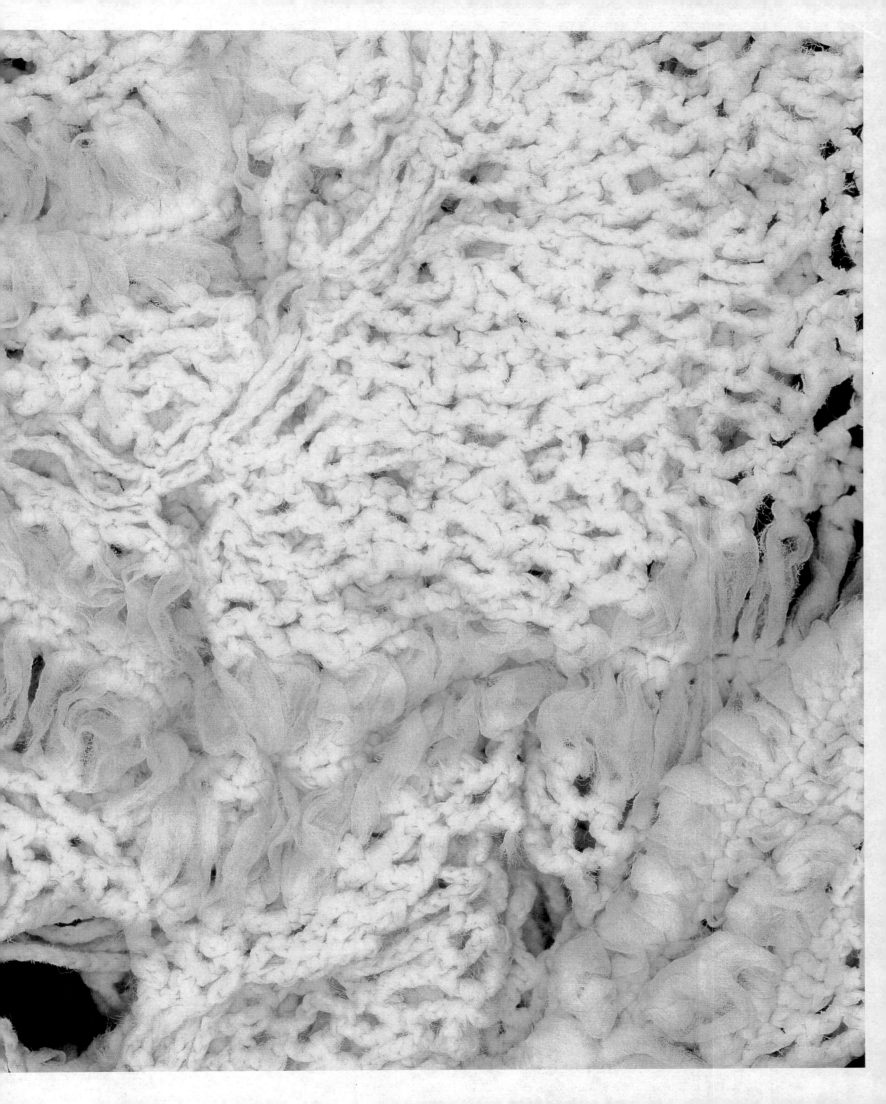

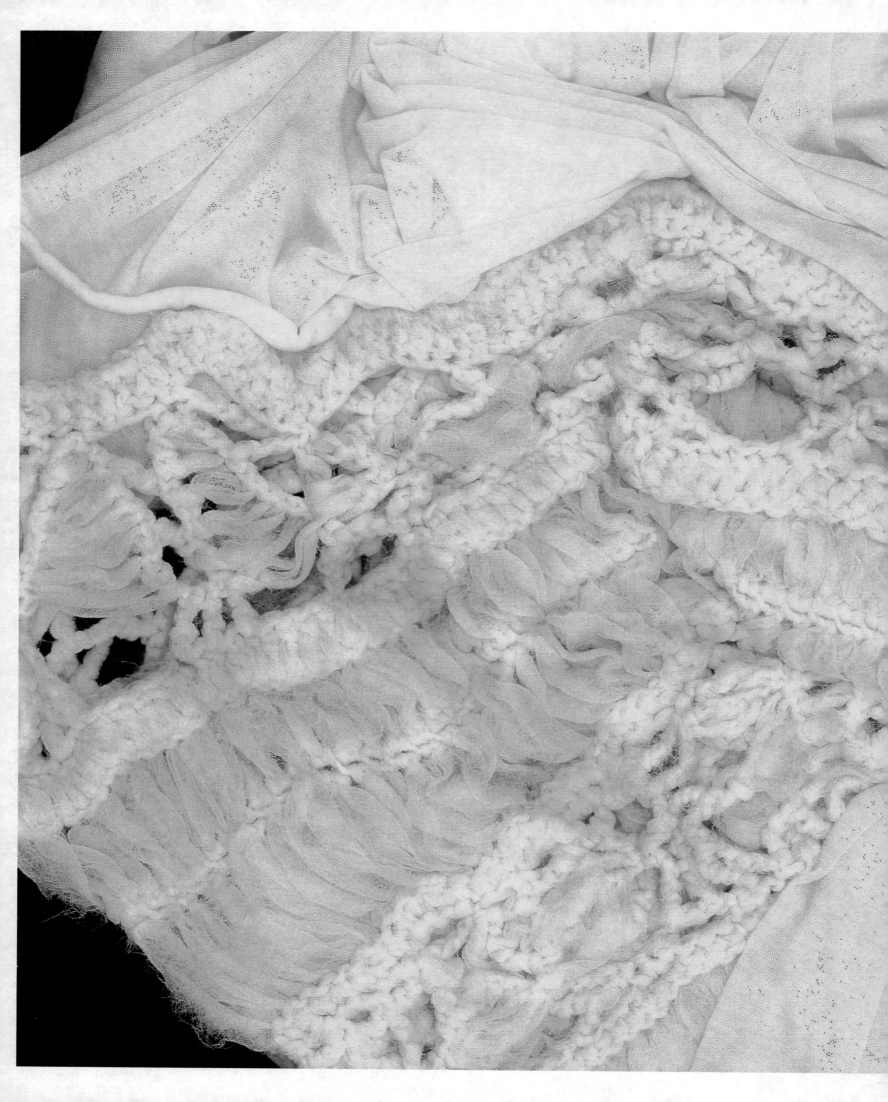

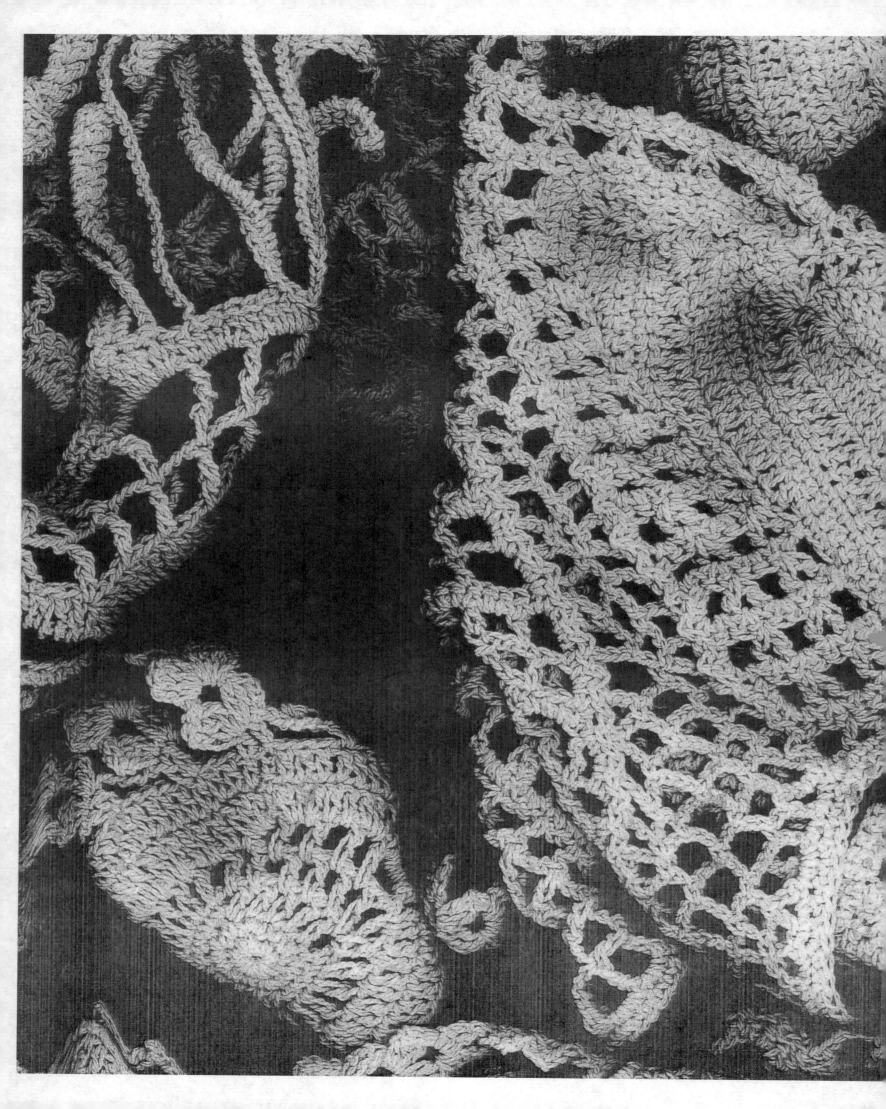

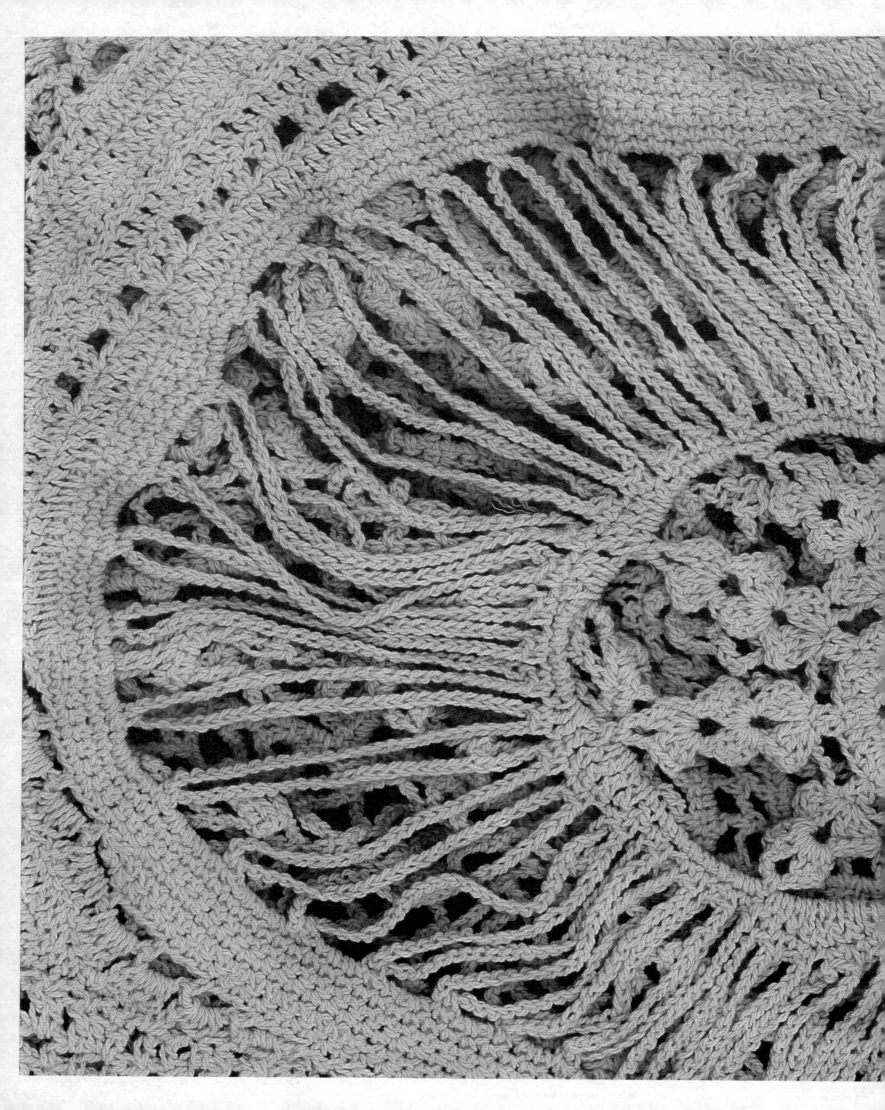

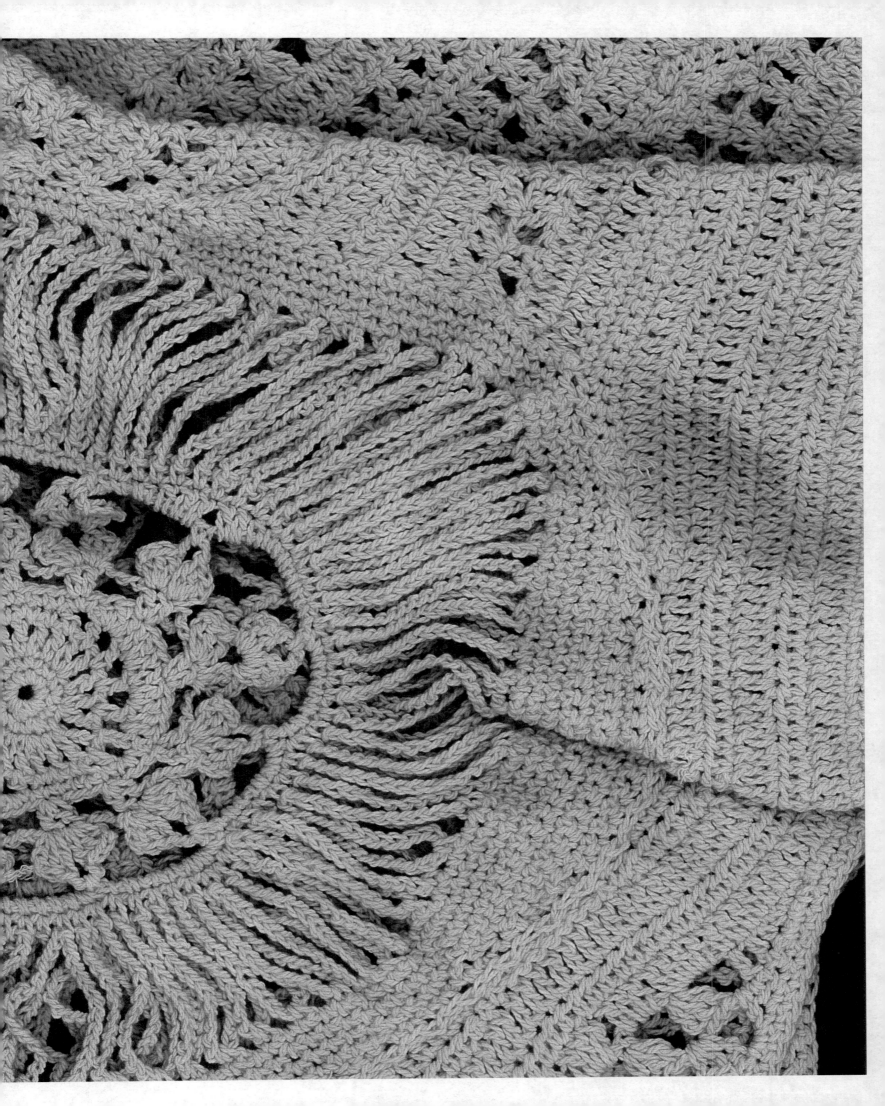

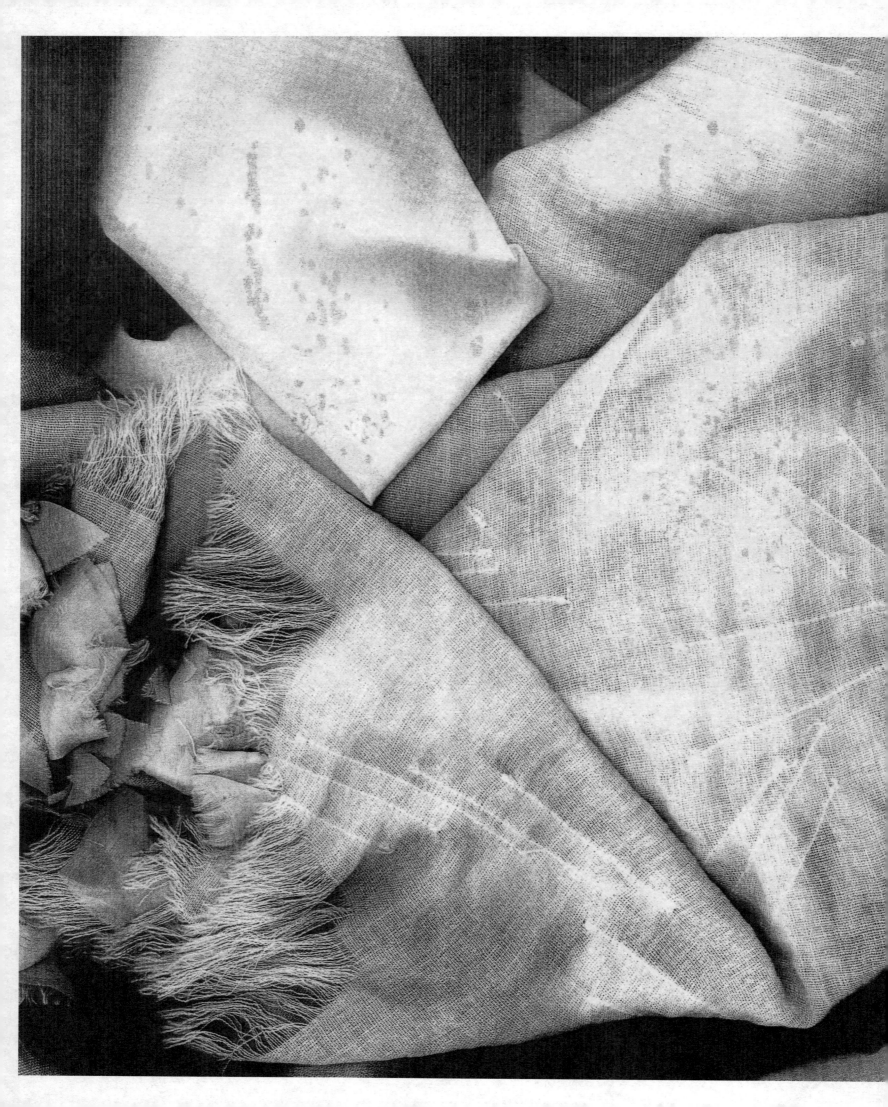

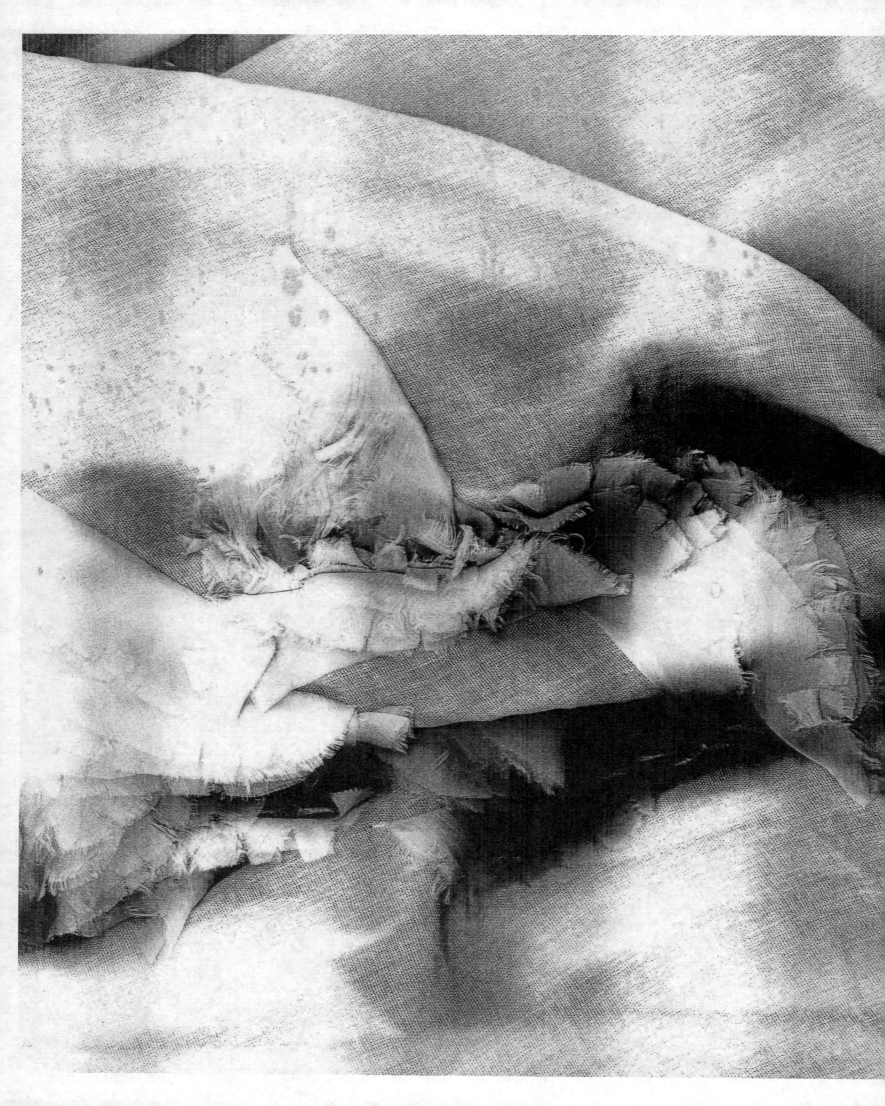

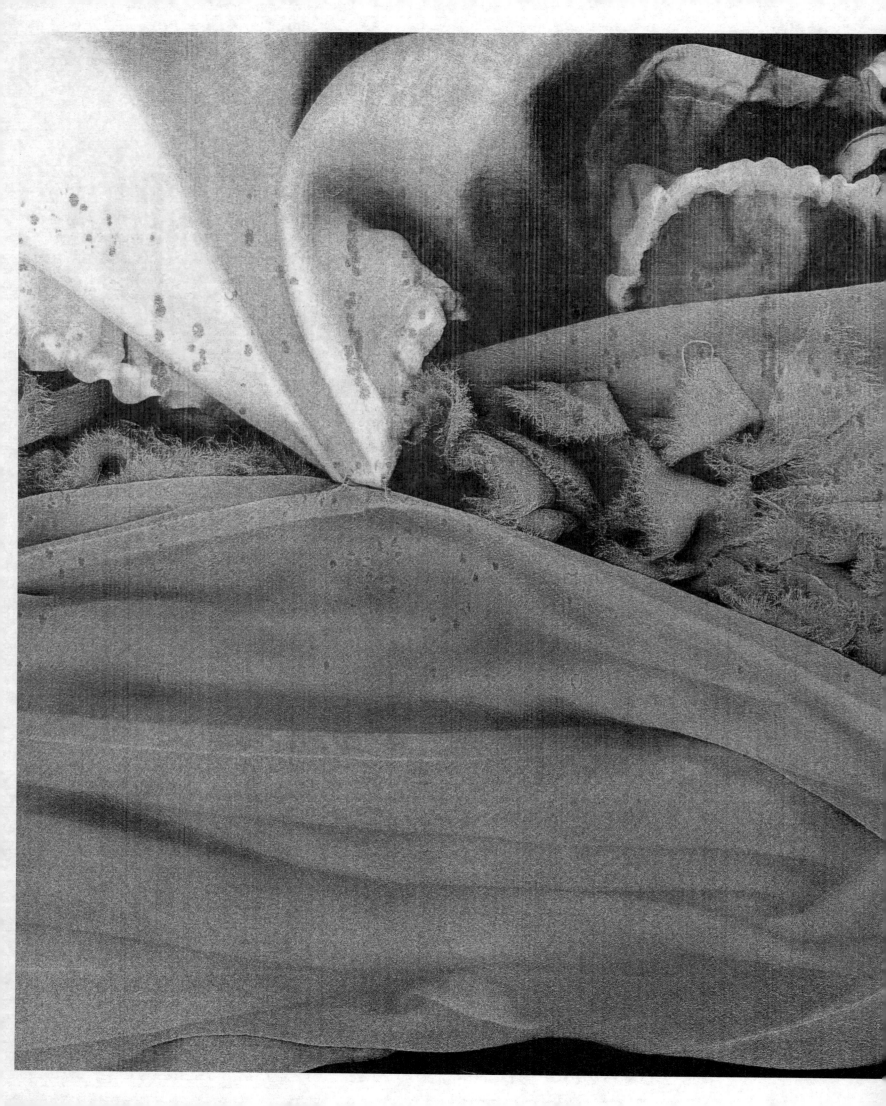

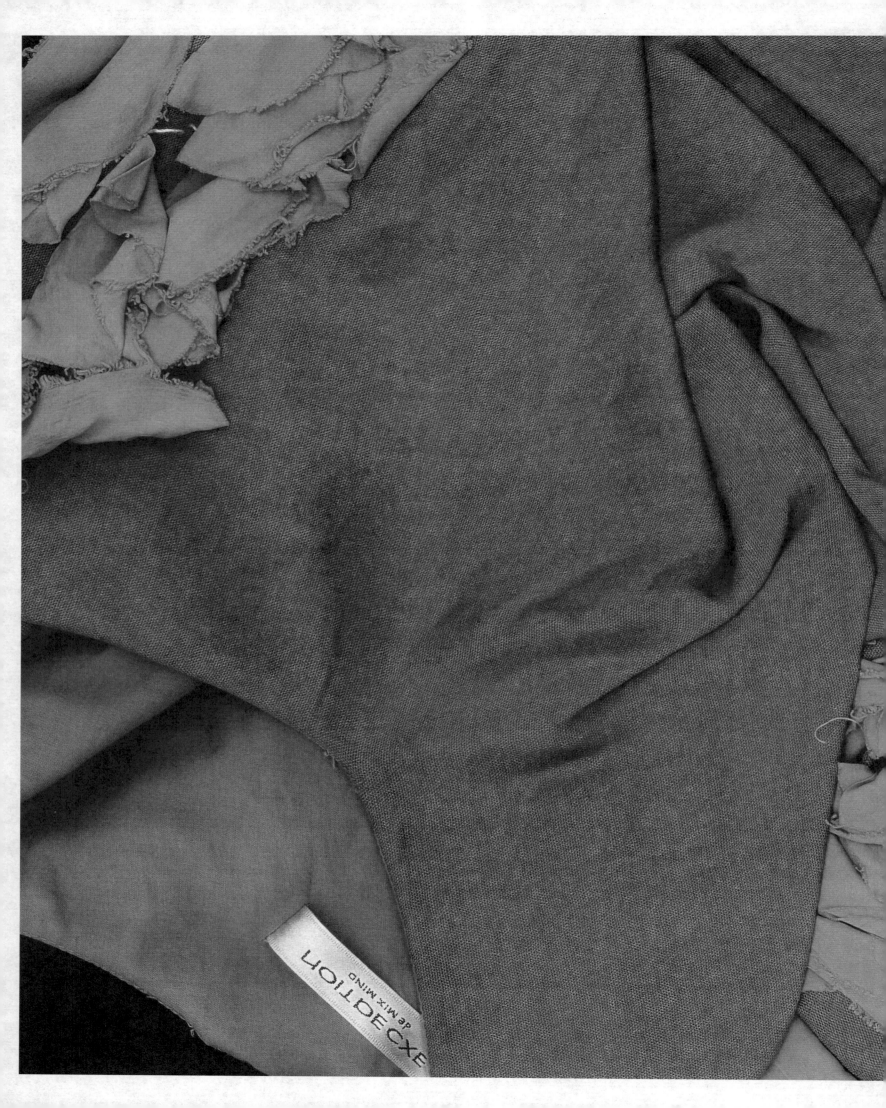

EXCEPTION
de MIX MIND

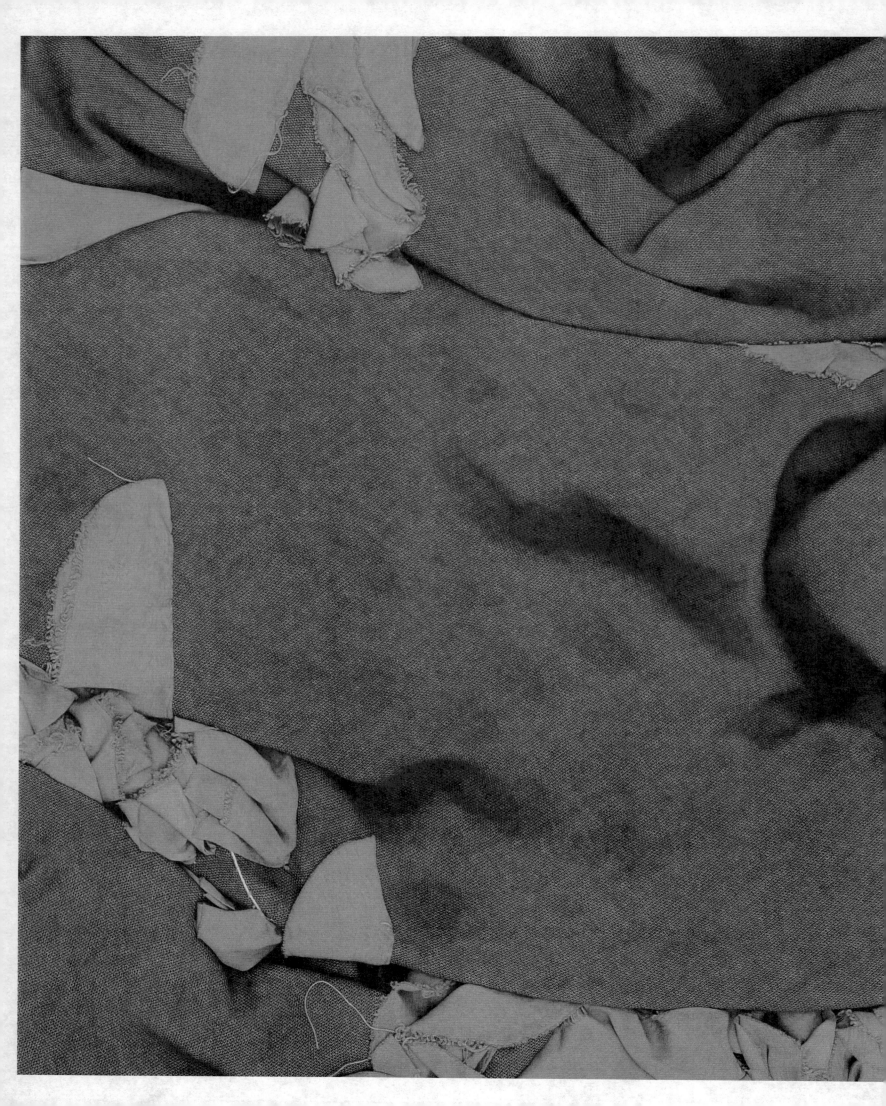

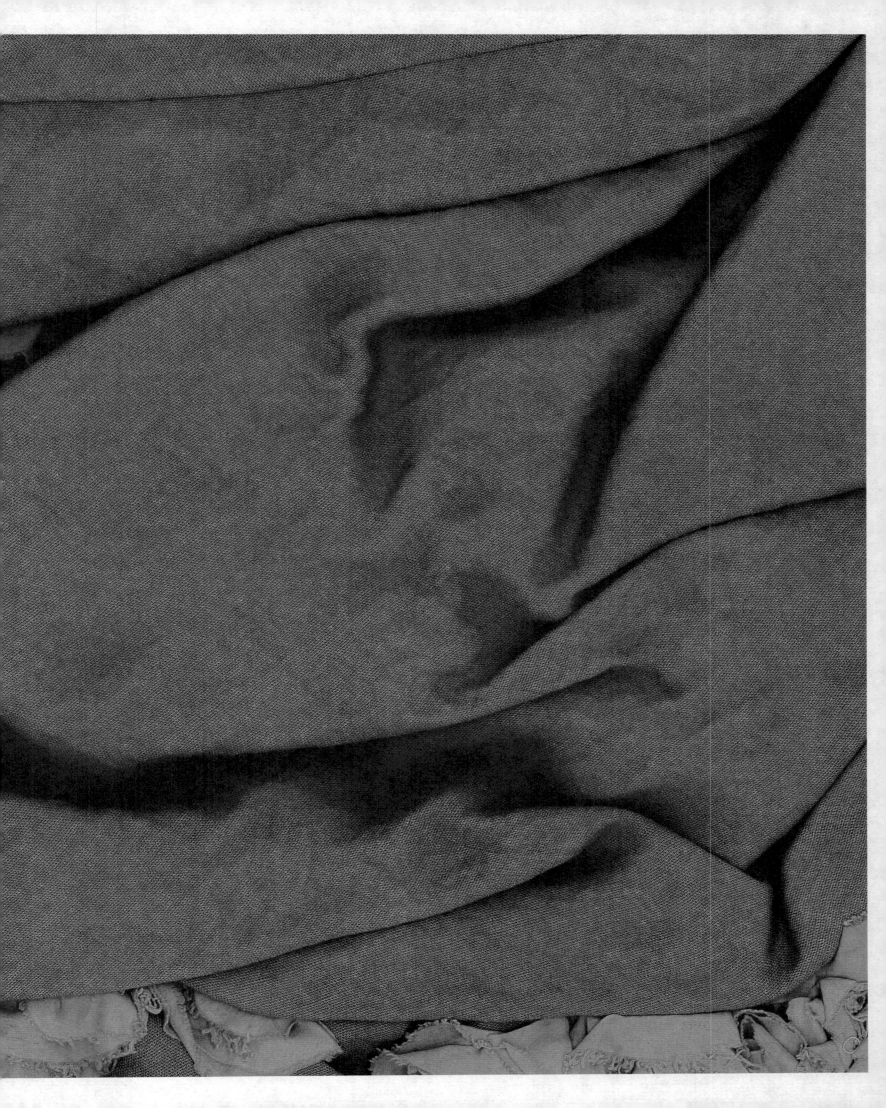

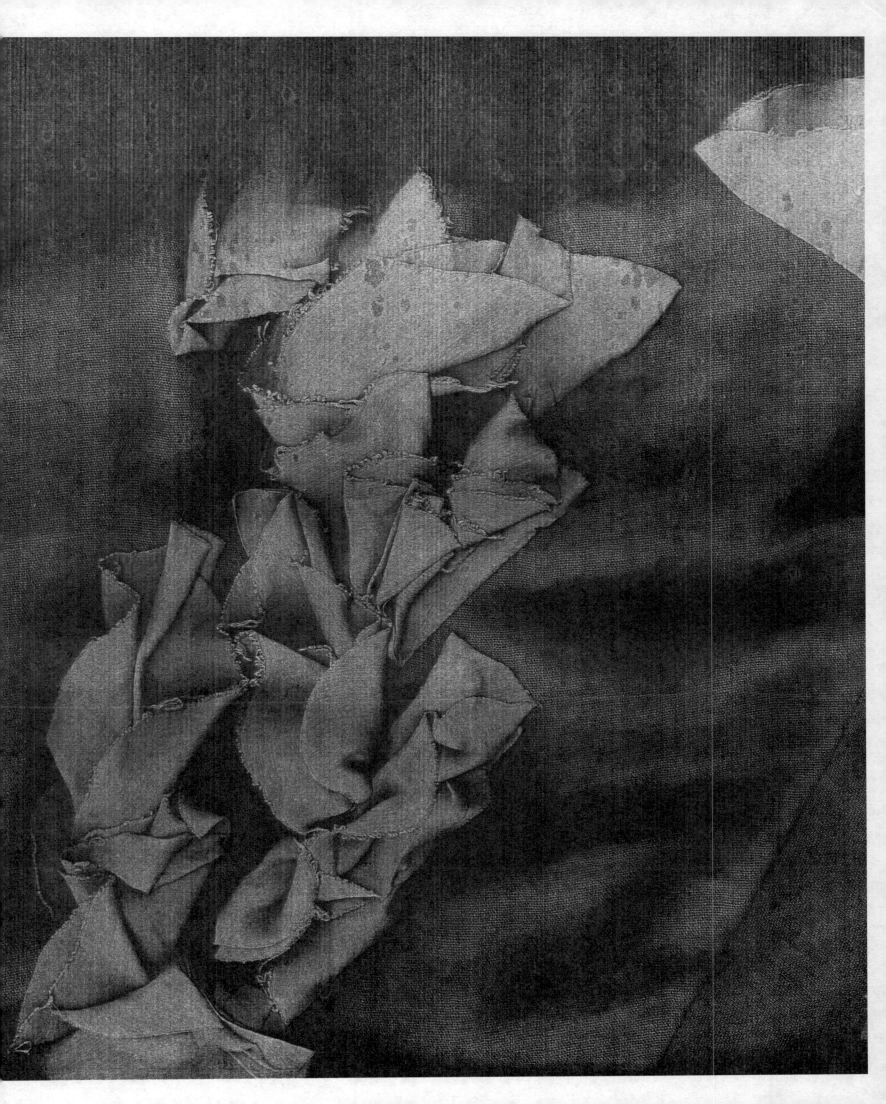

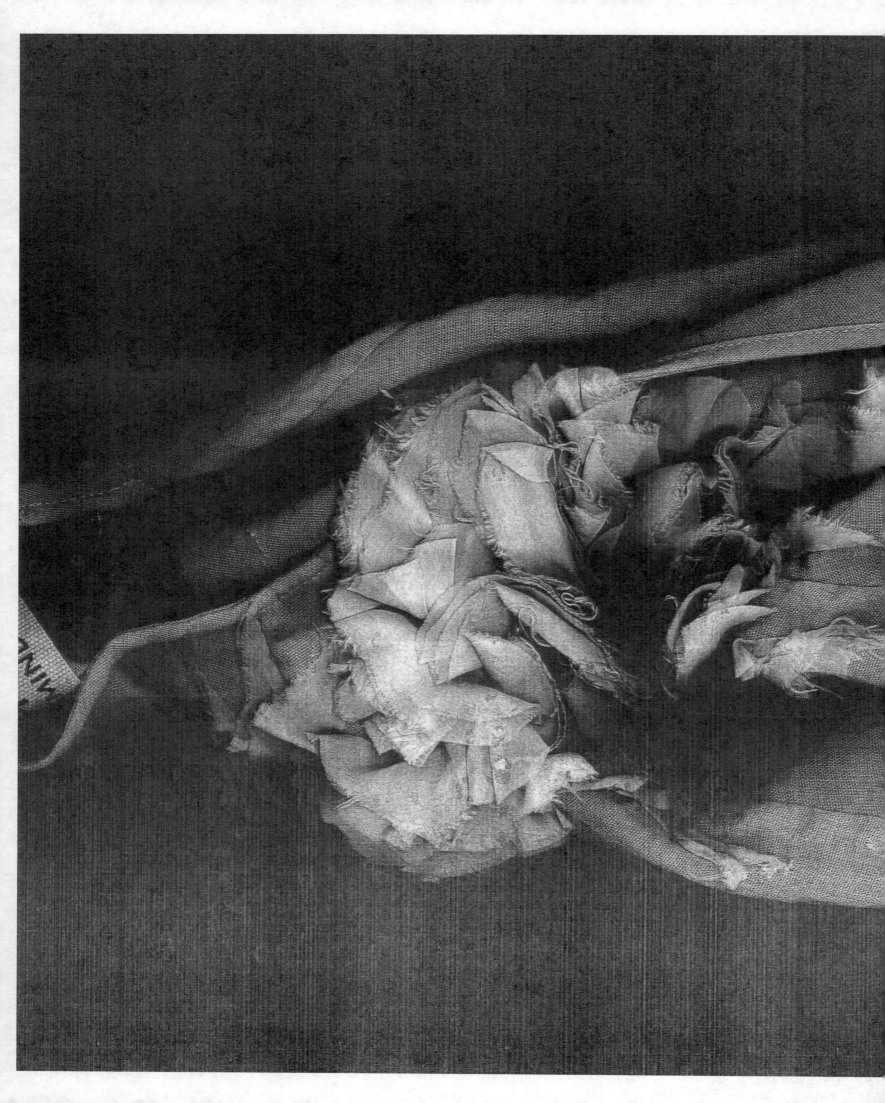

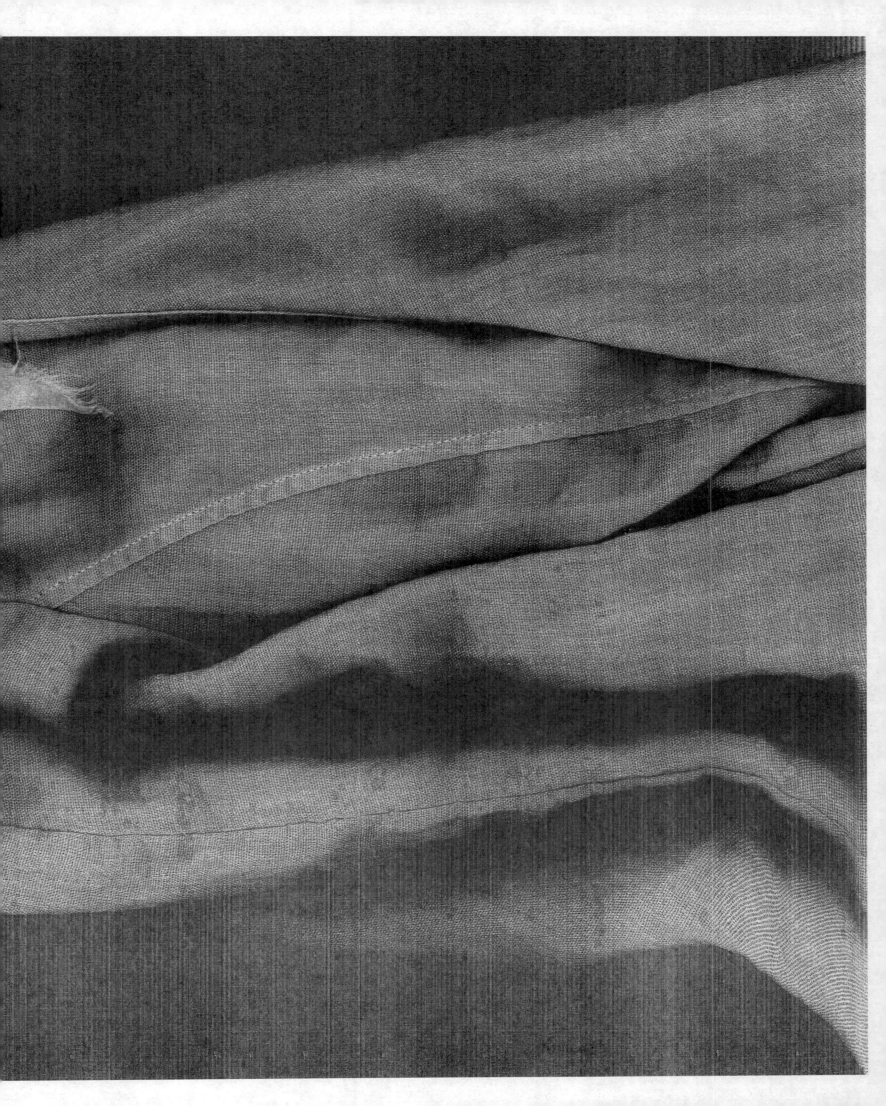

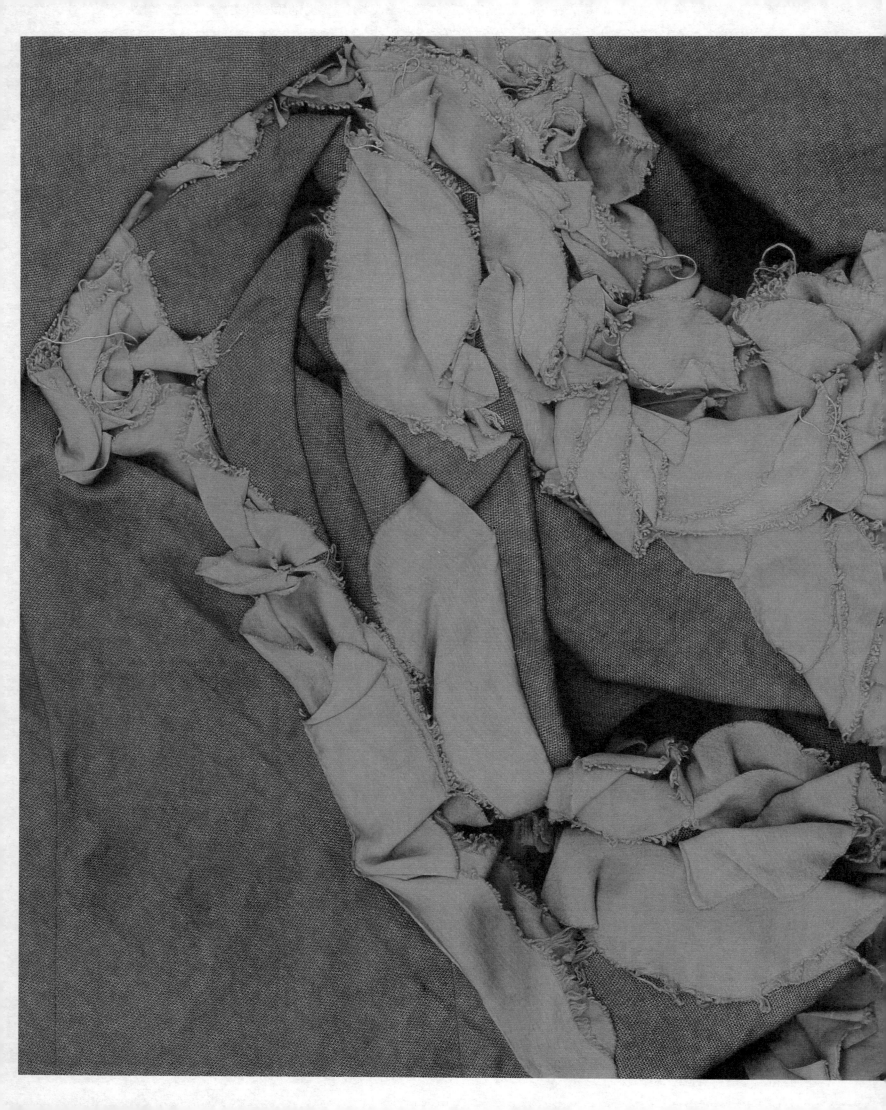

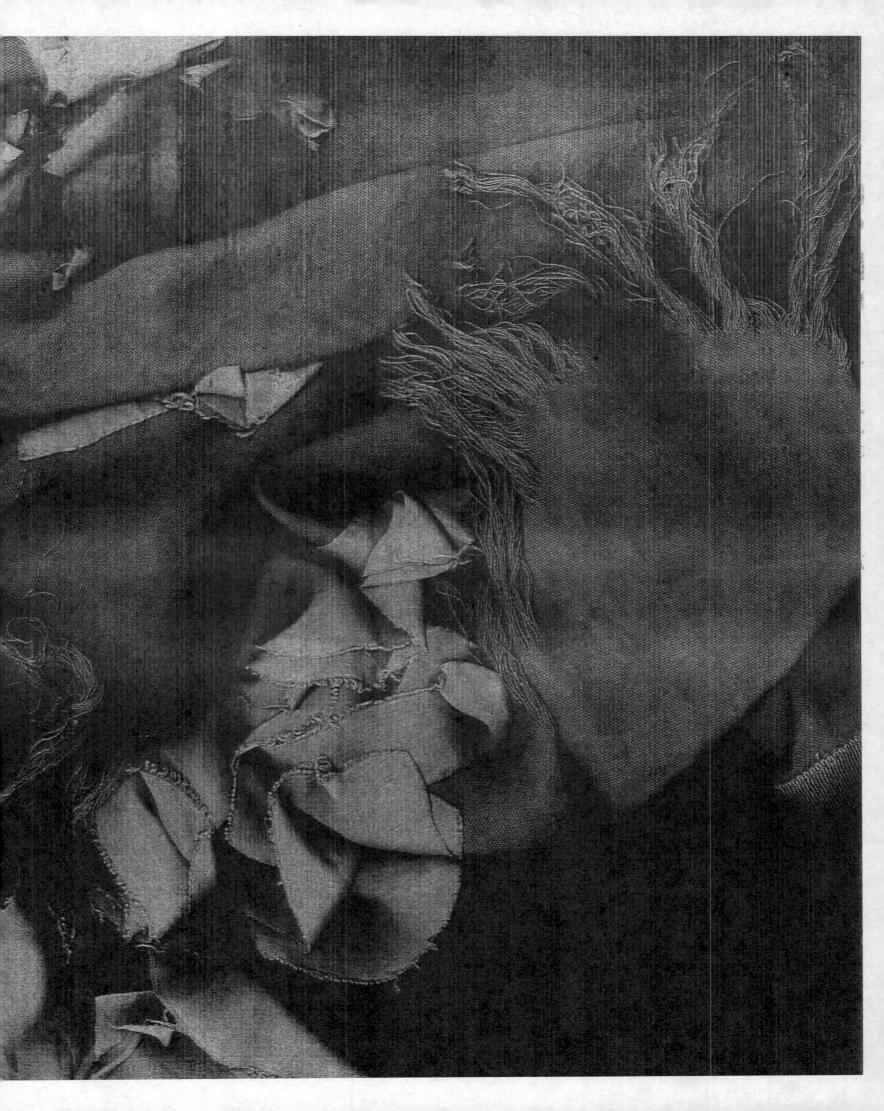

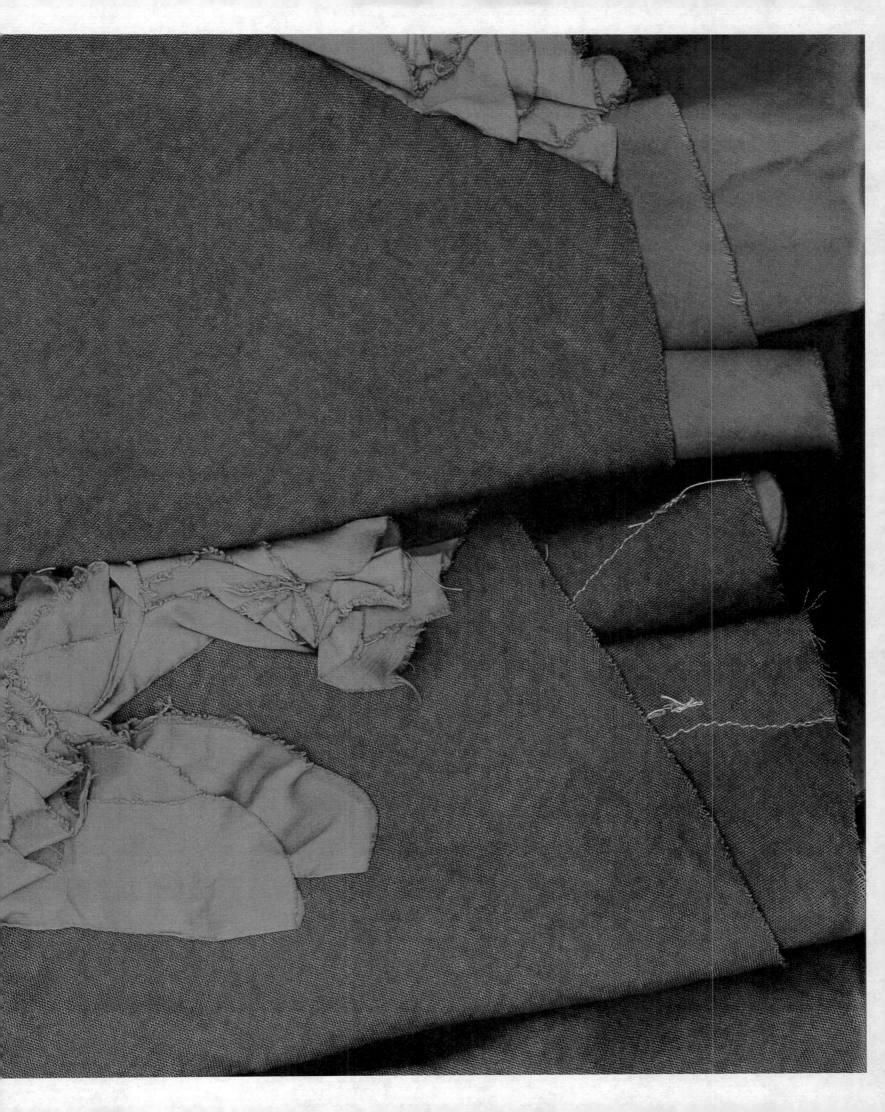

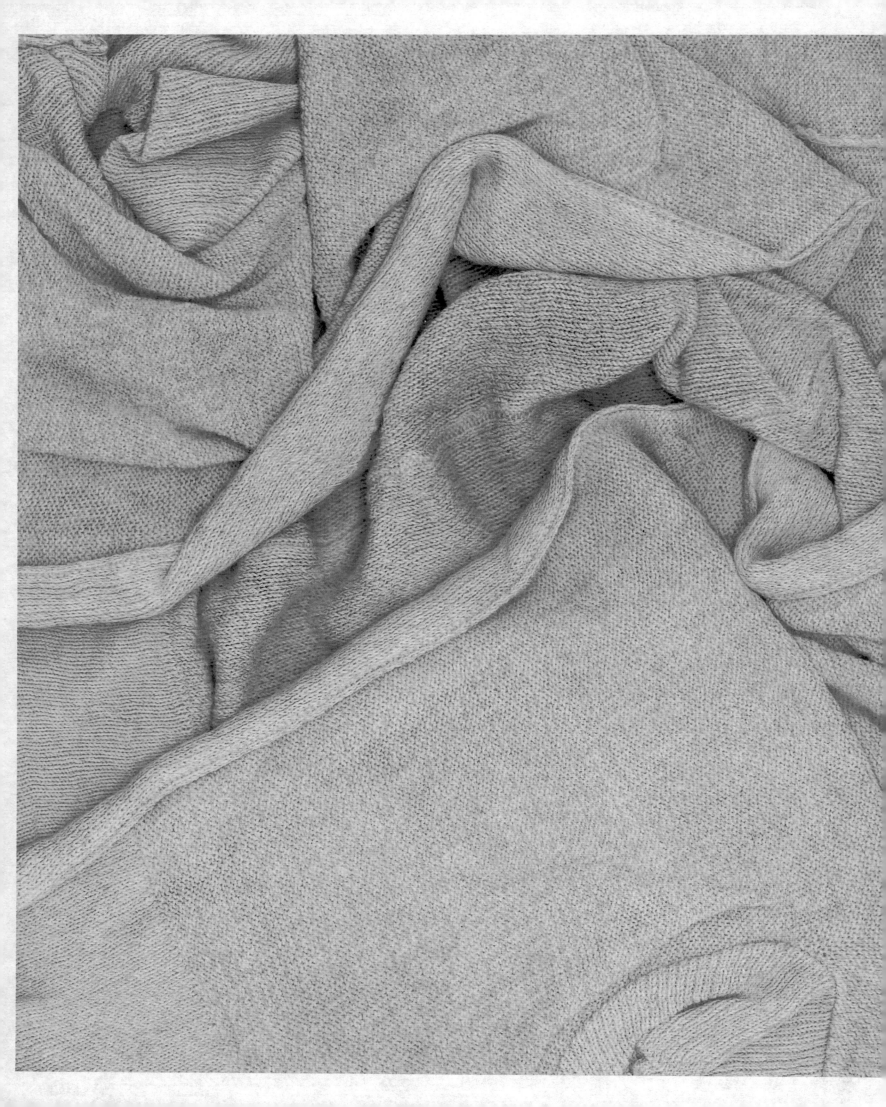

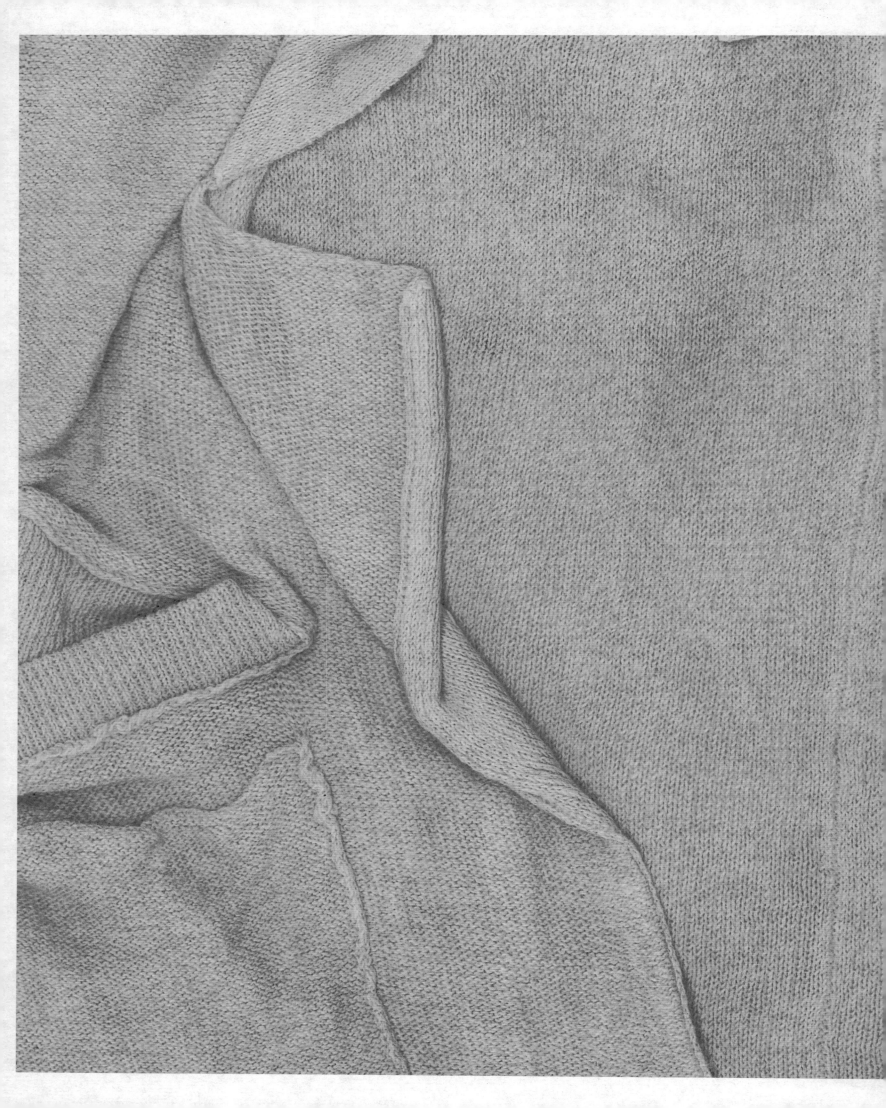

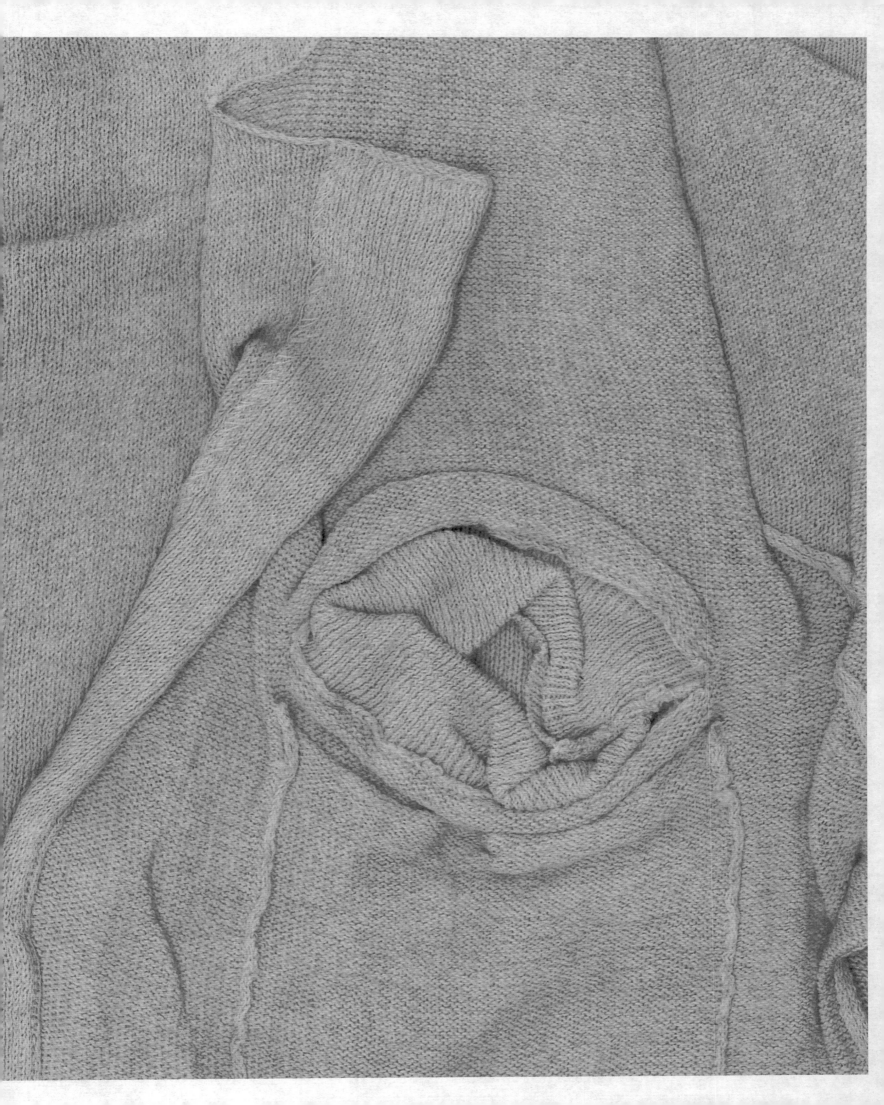

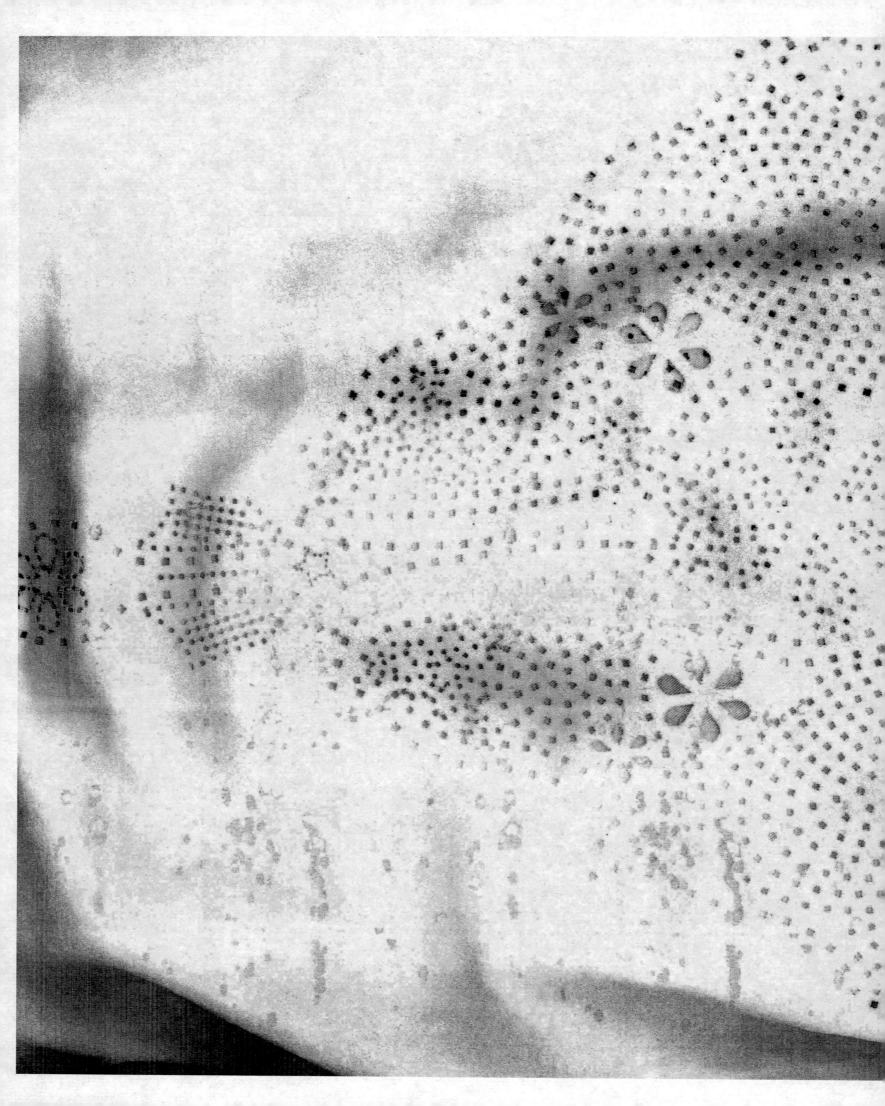

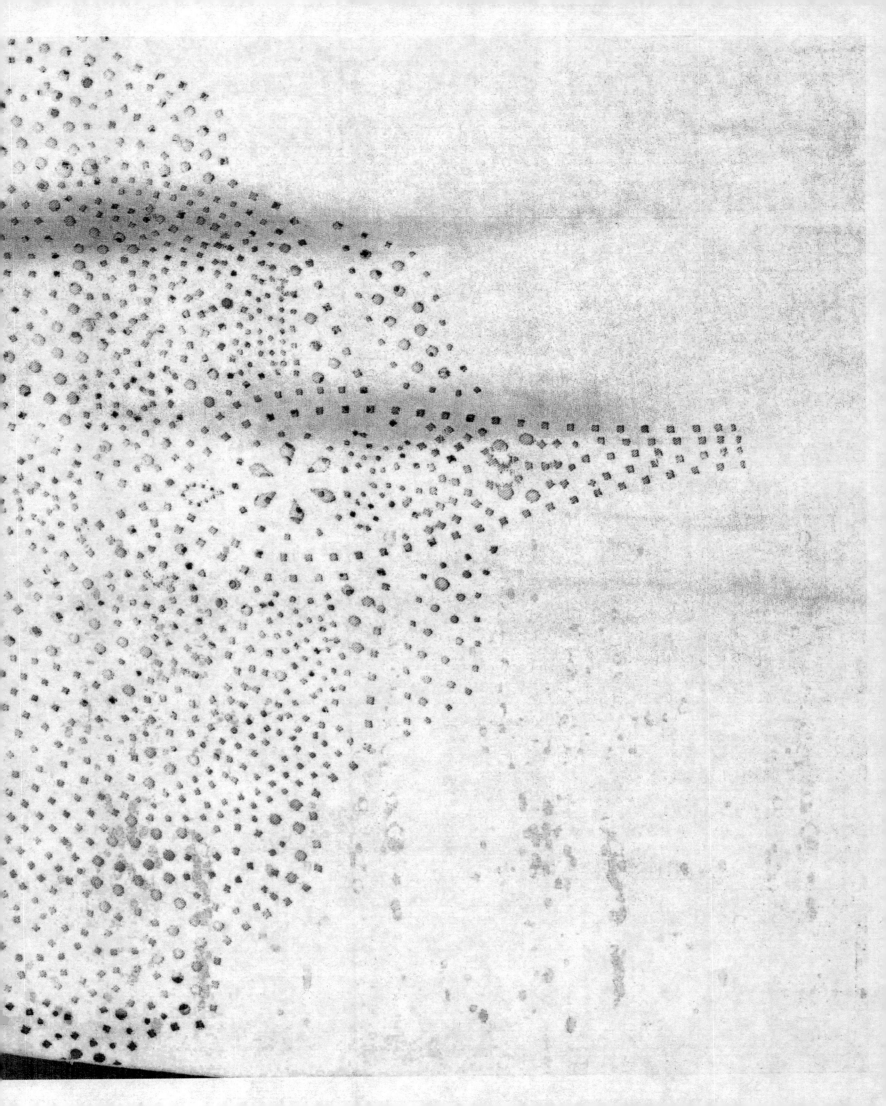

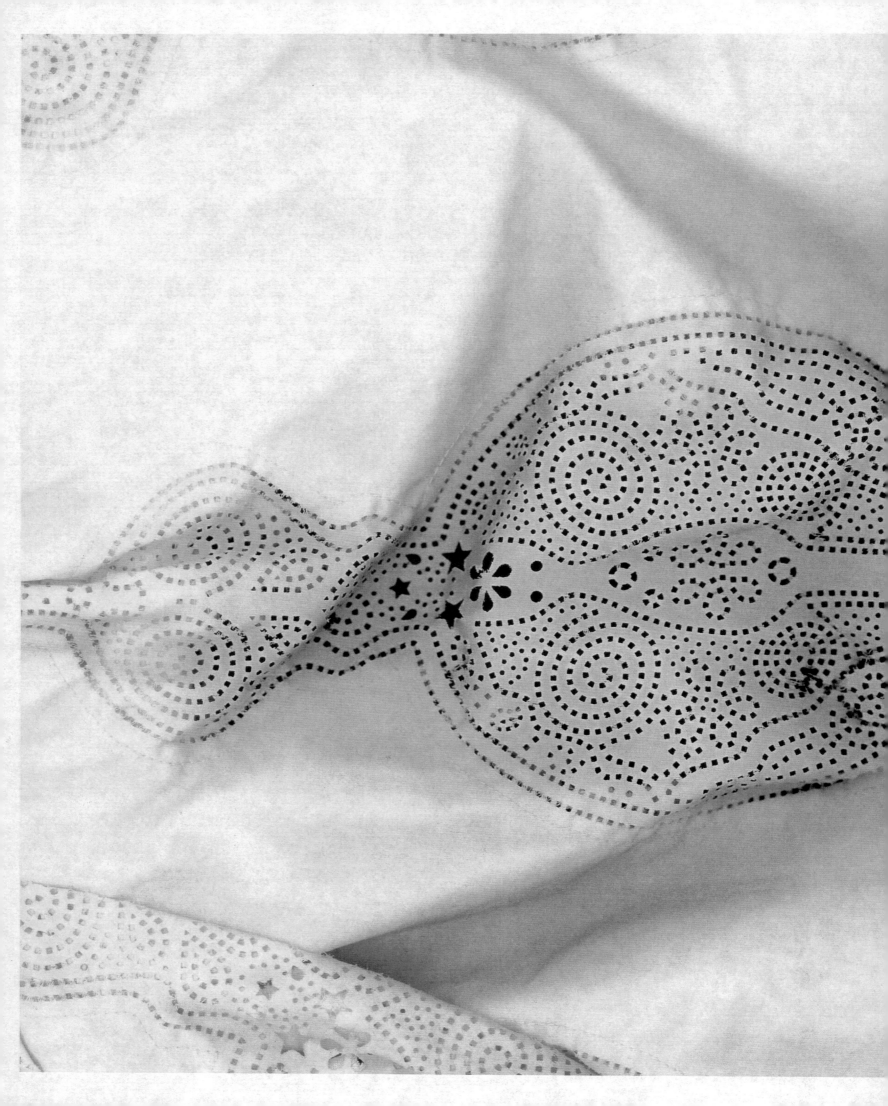

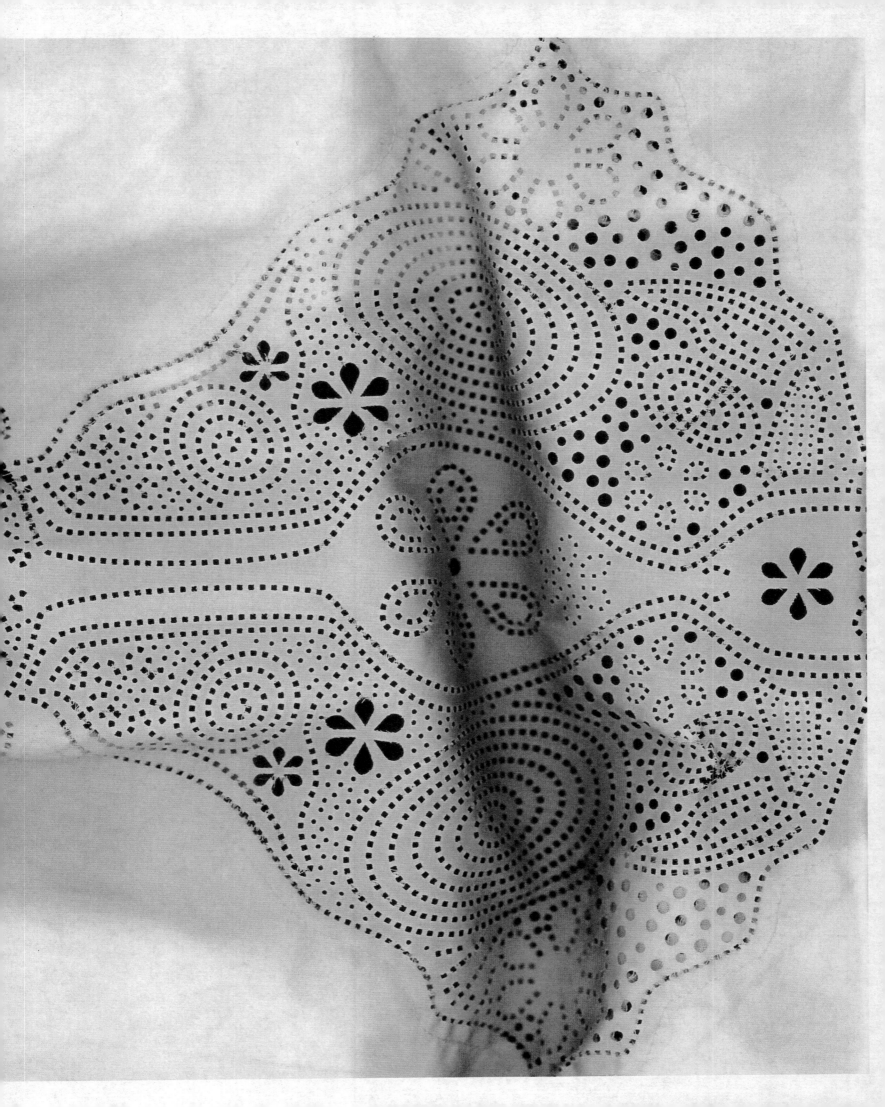

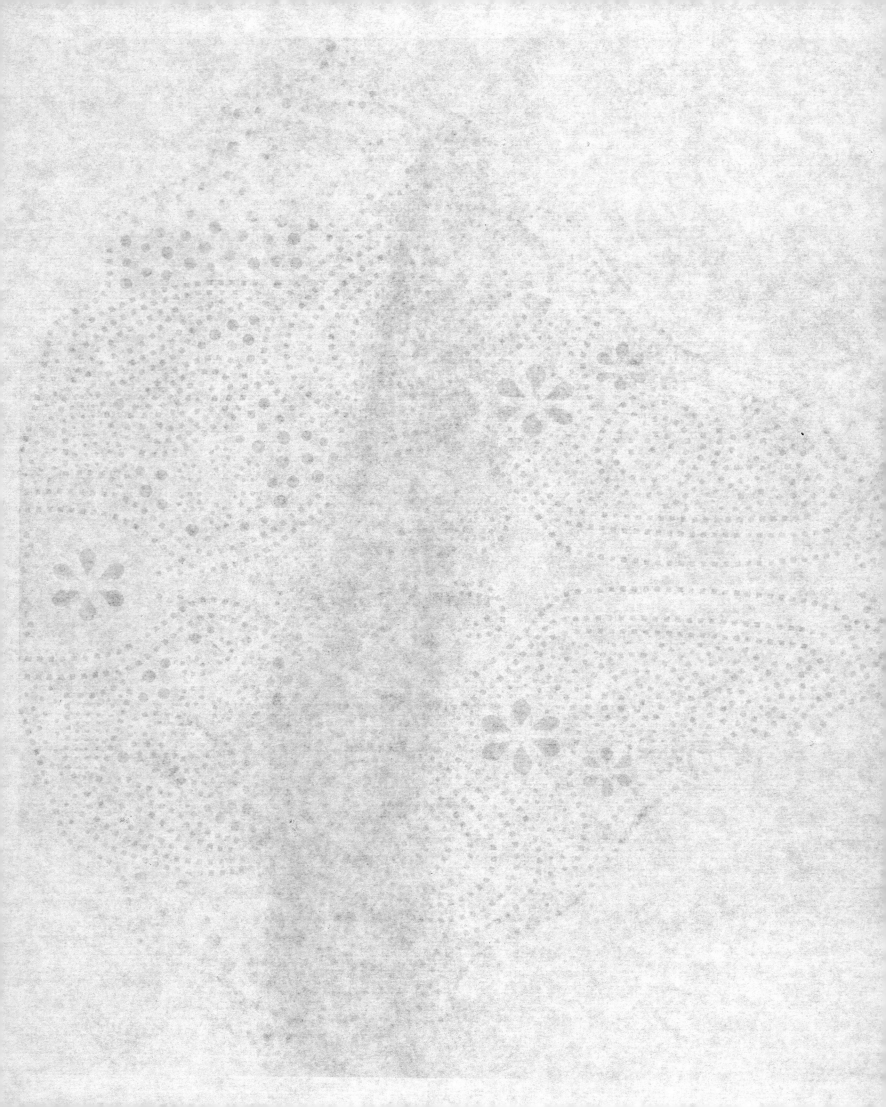

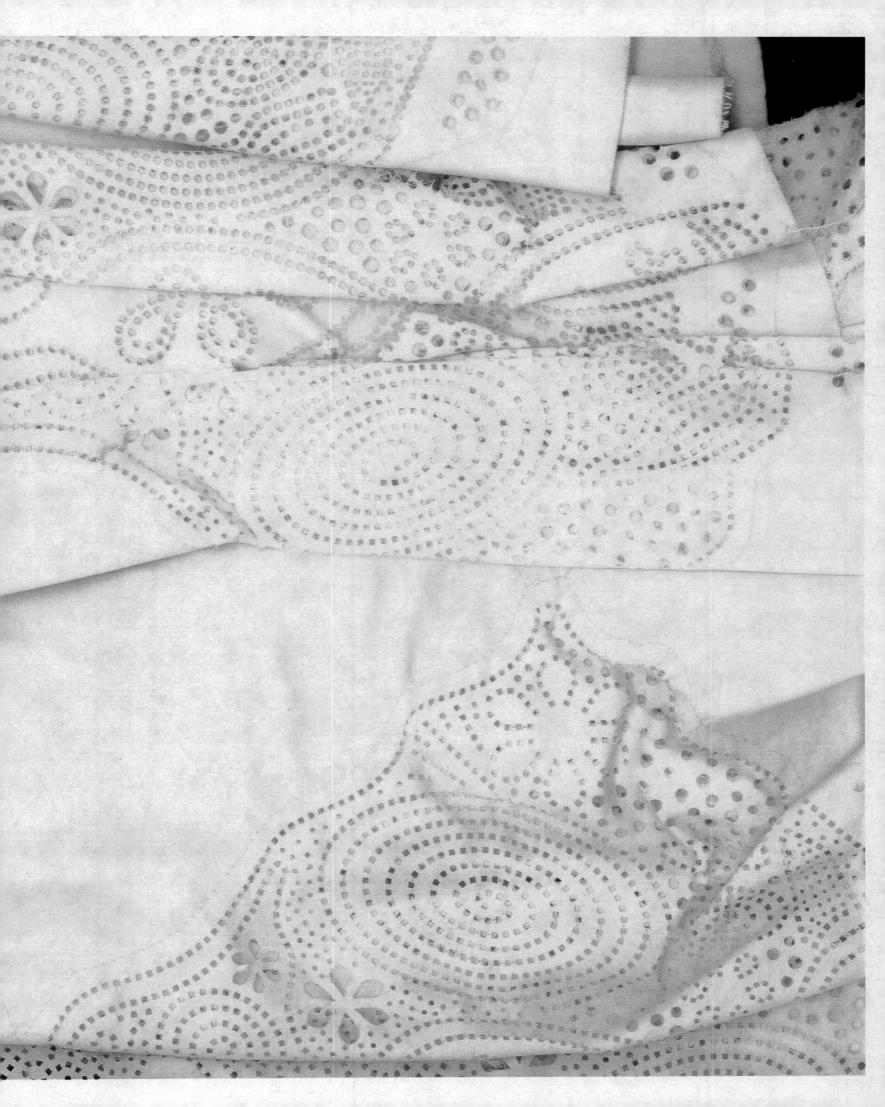

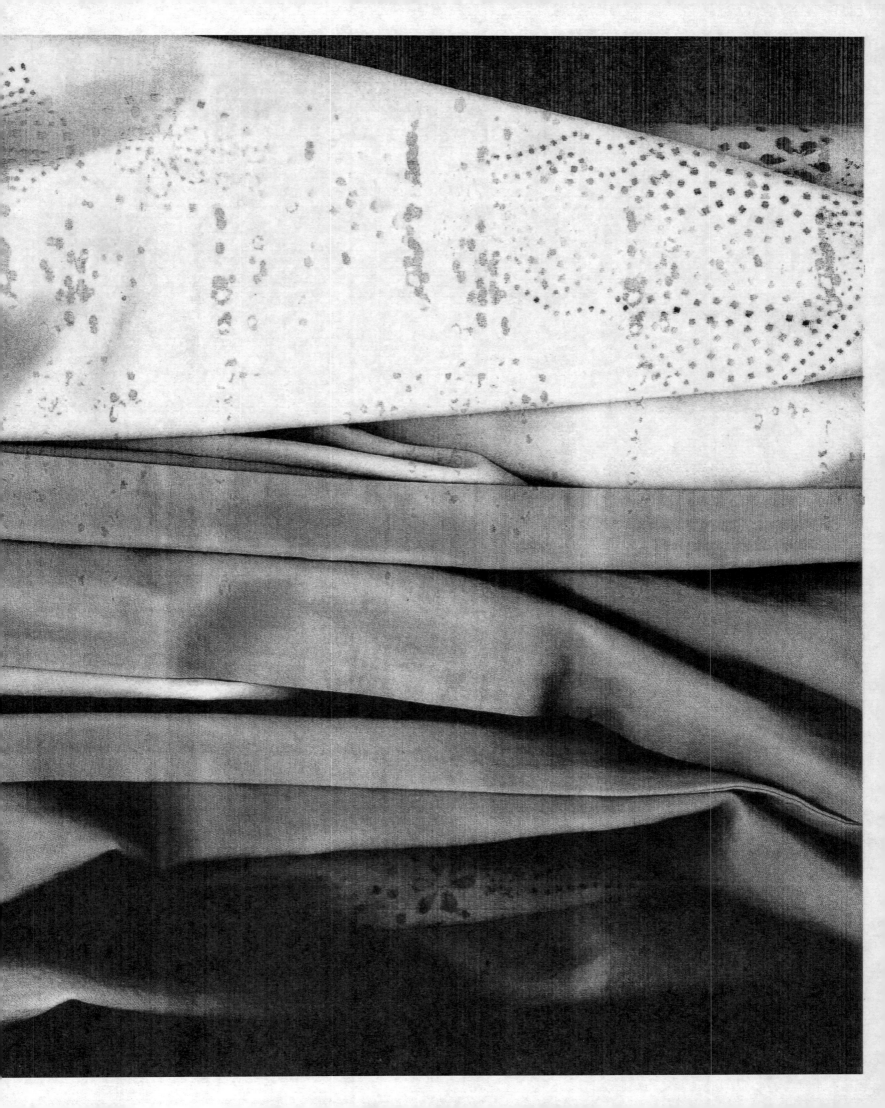

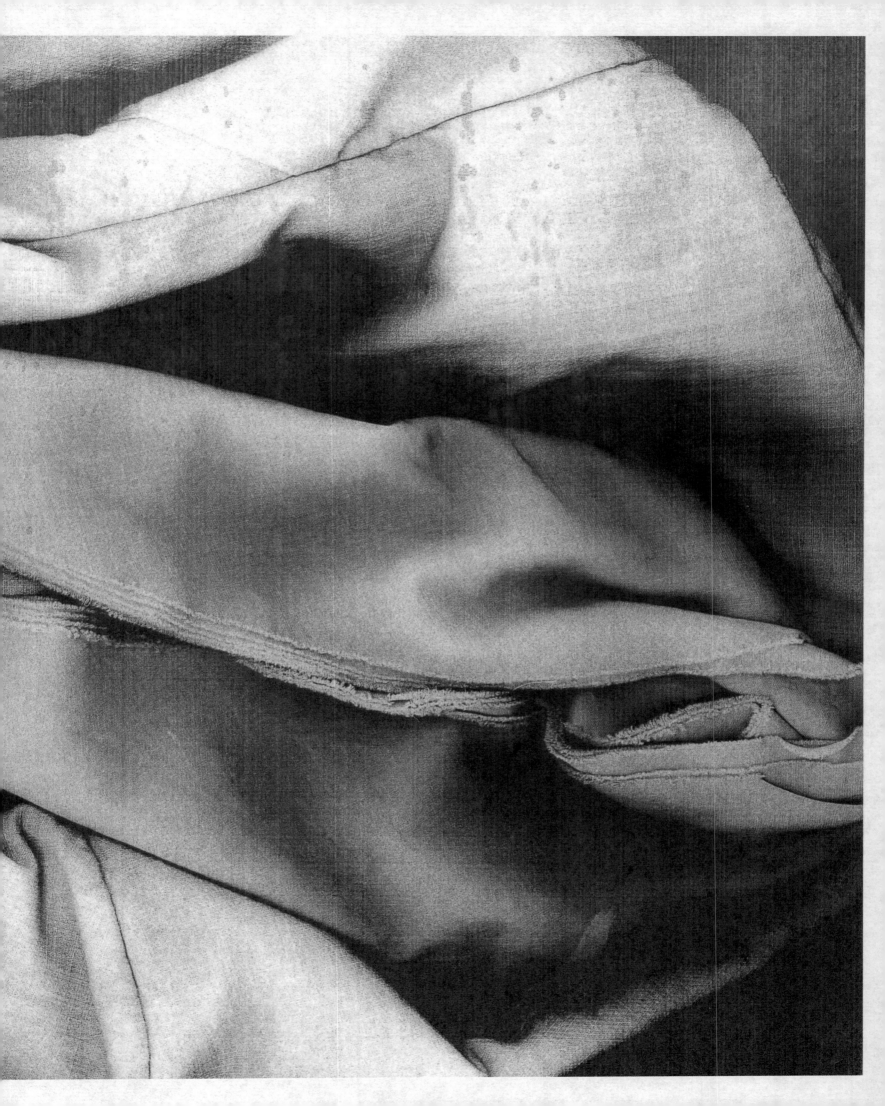

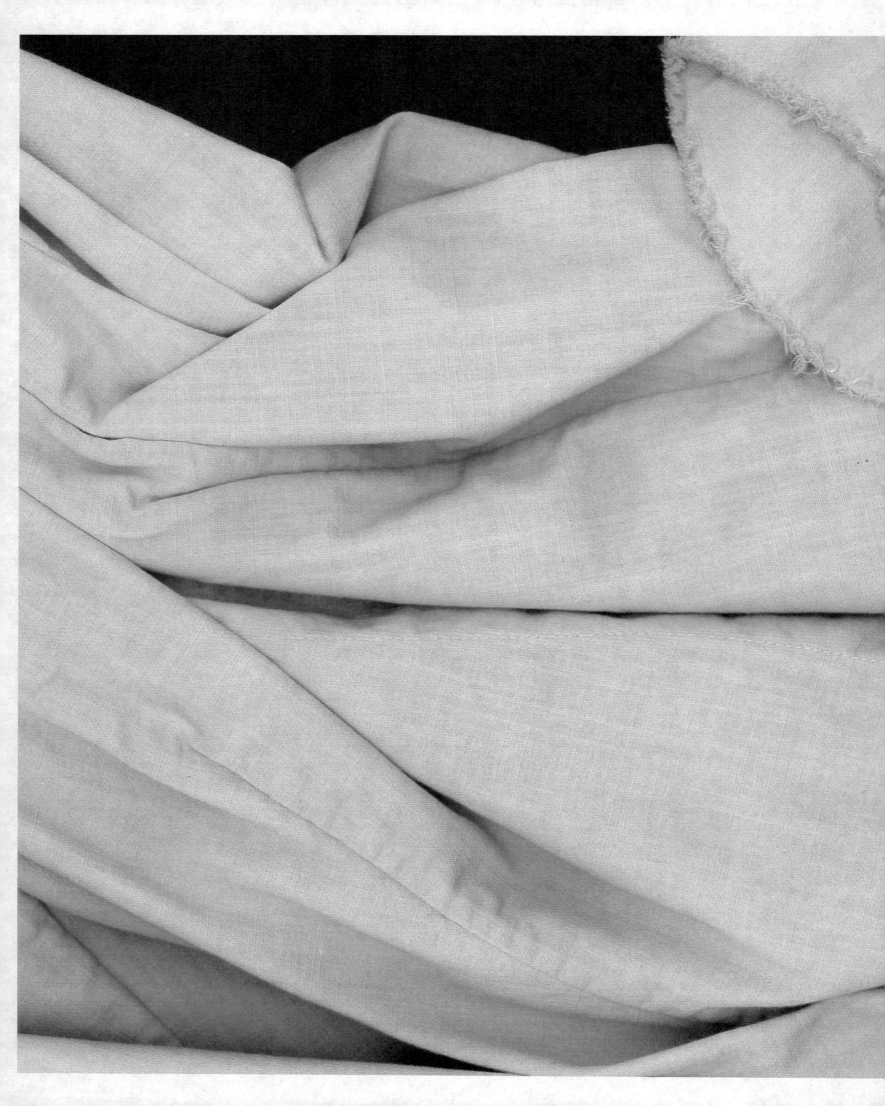

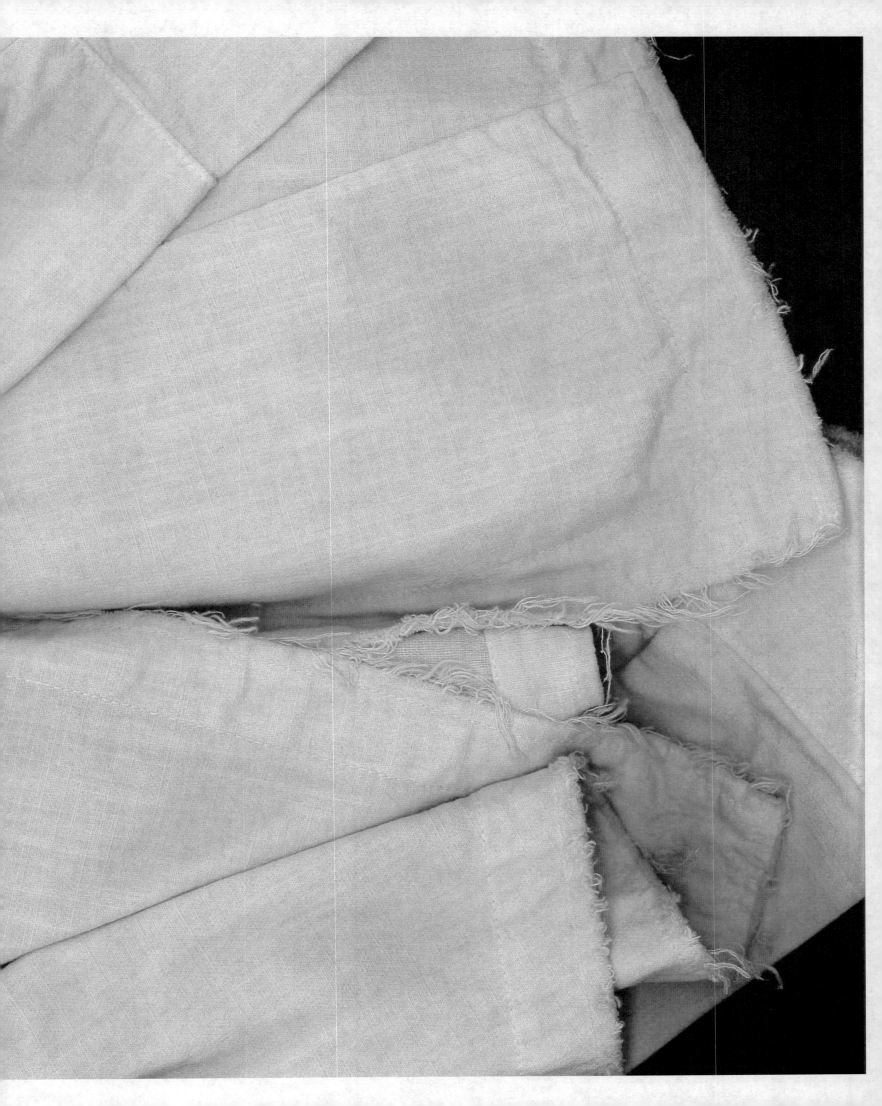

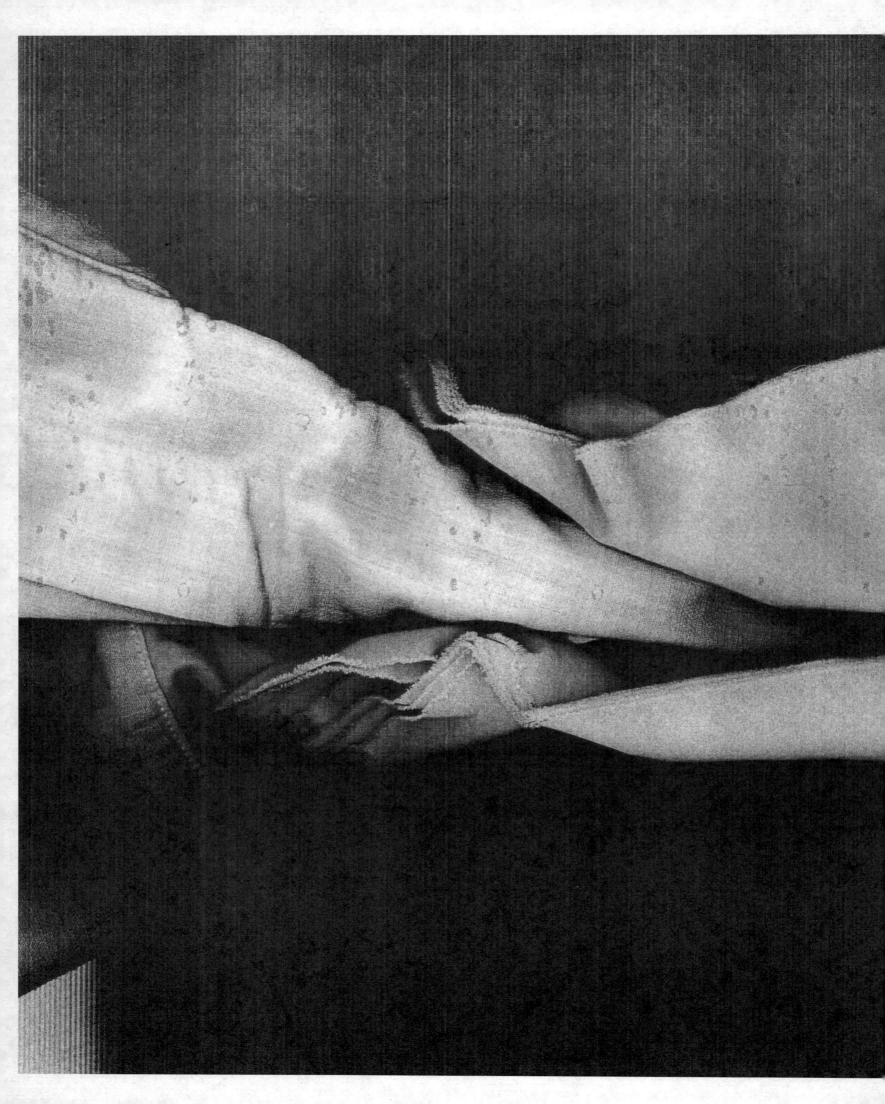

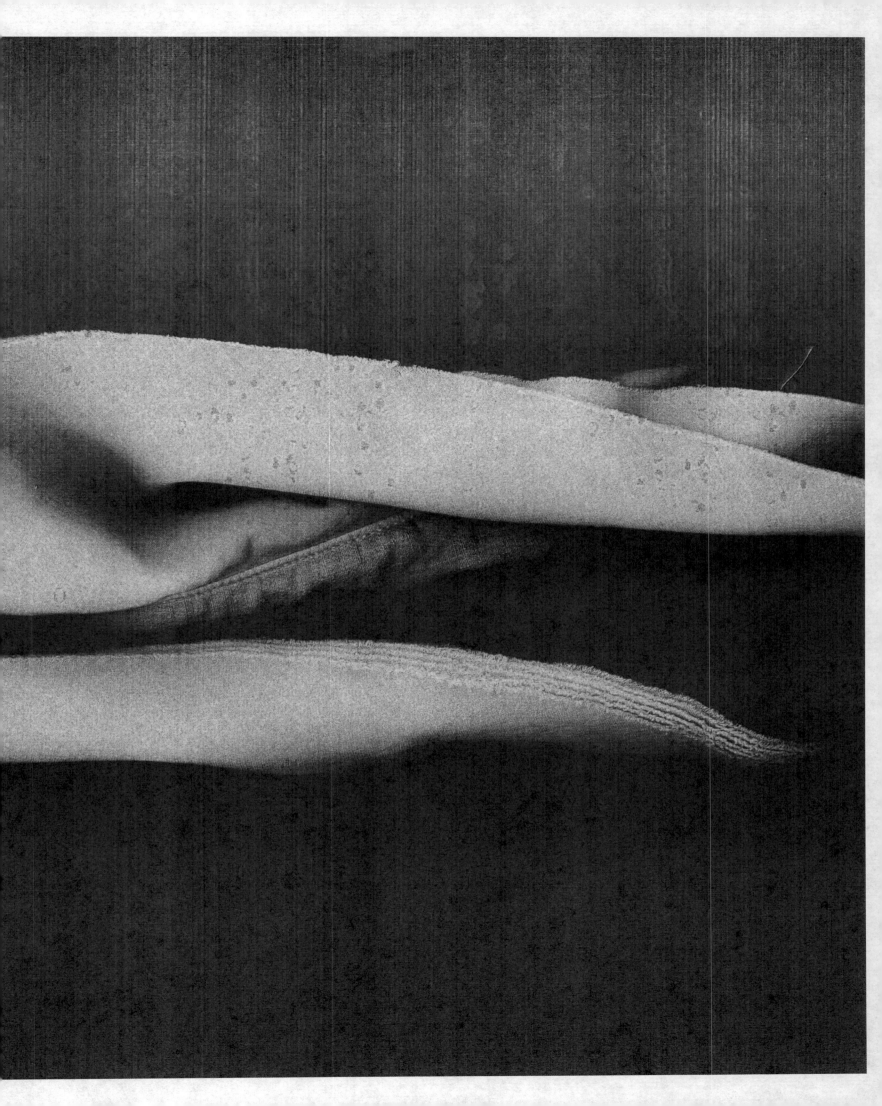

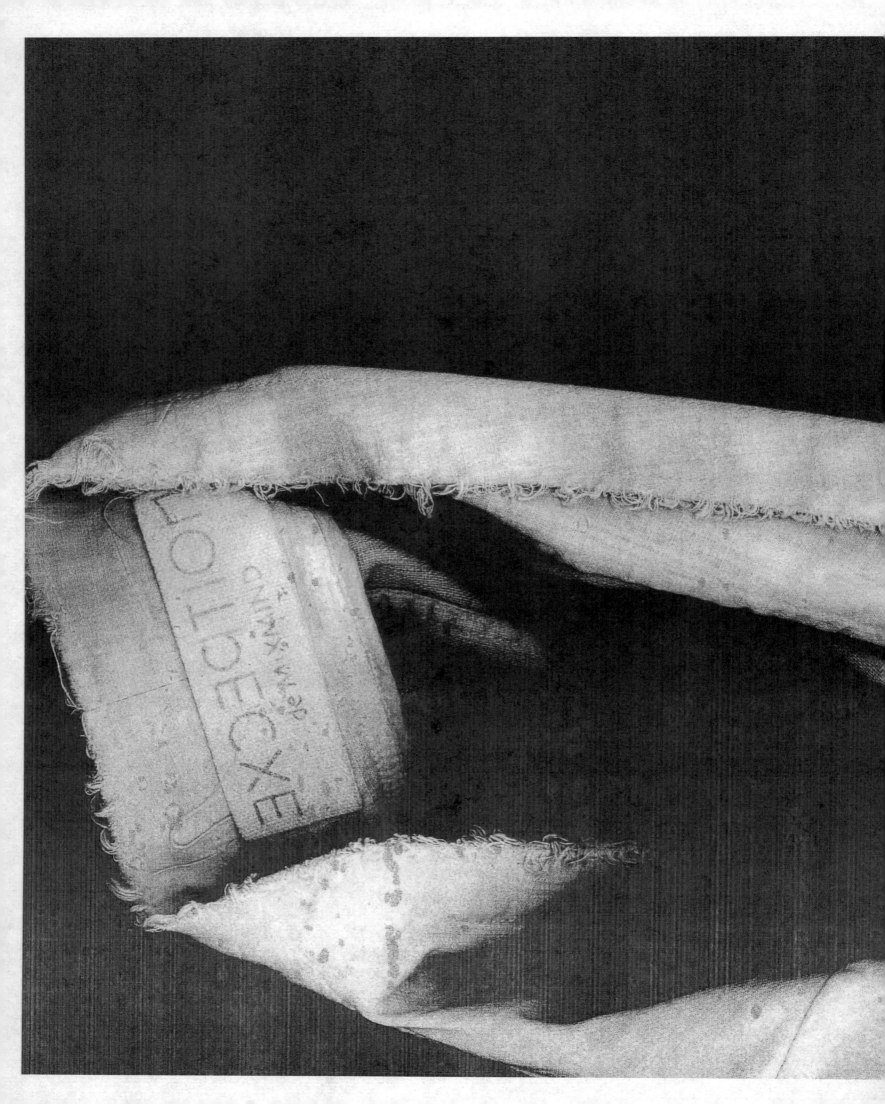

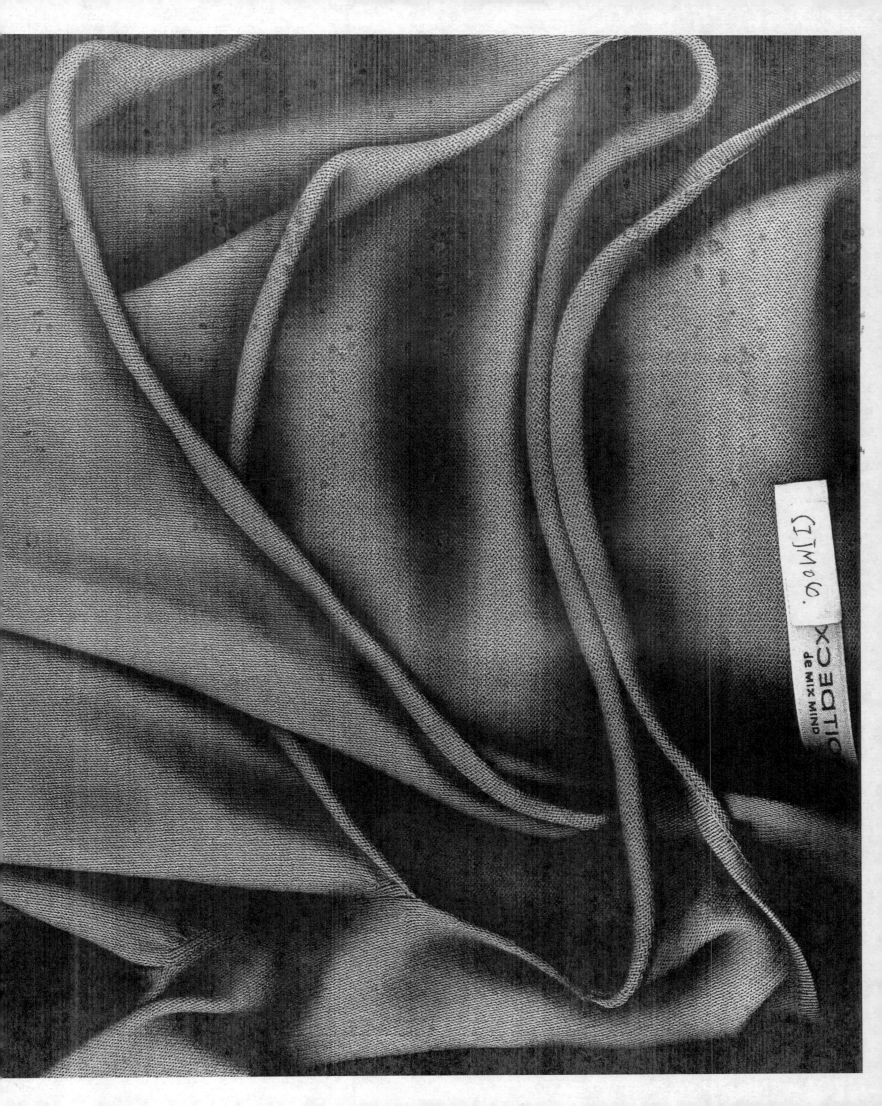

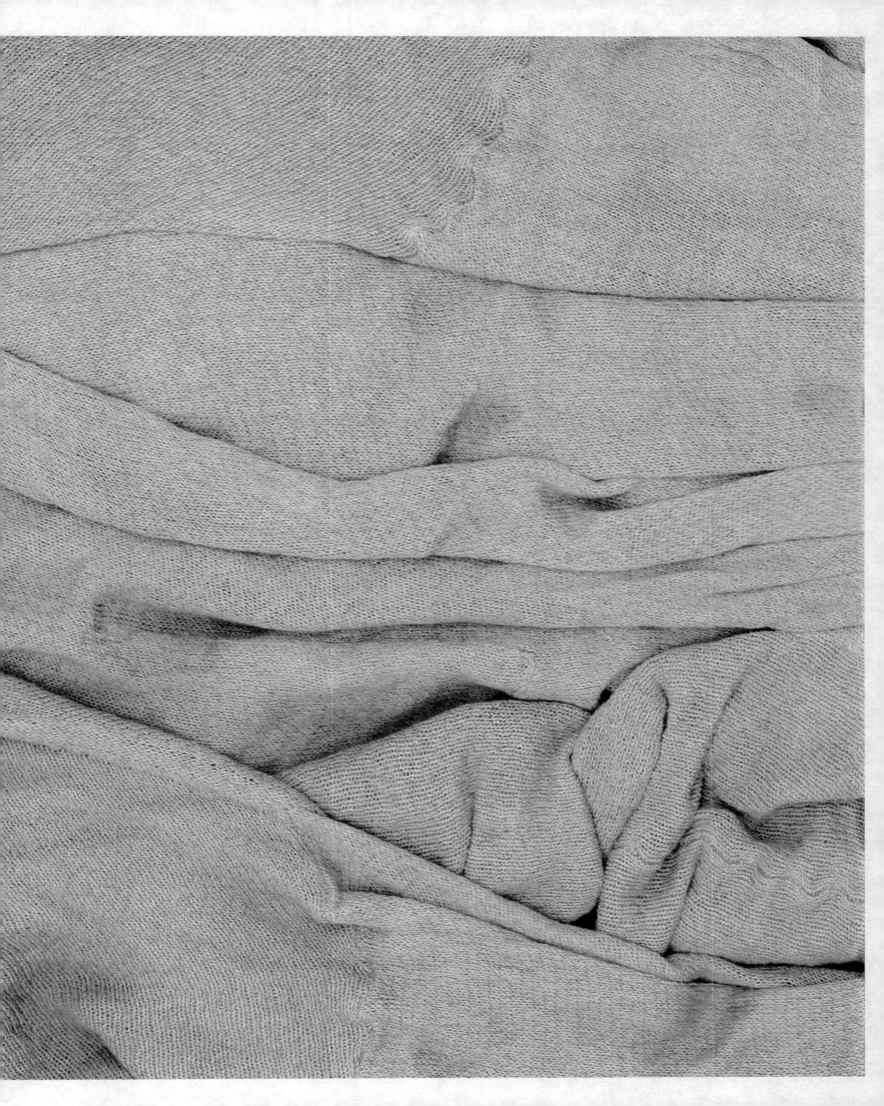

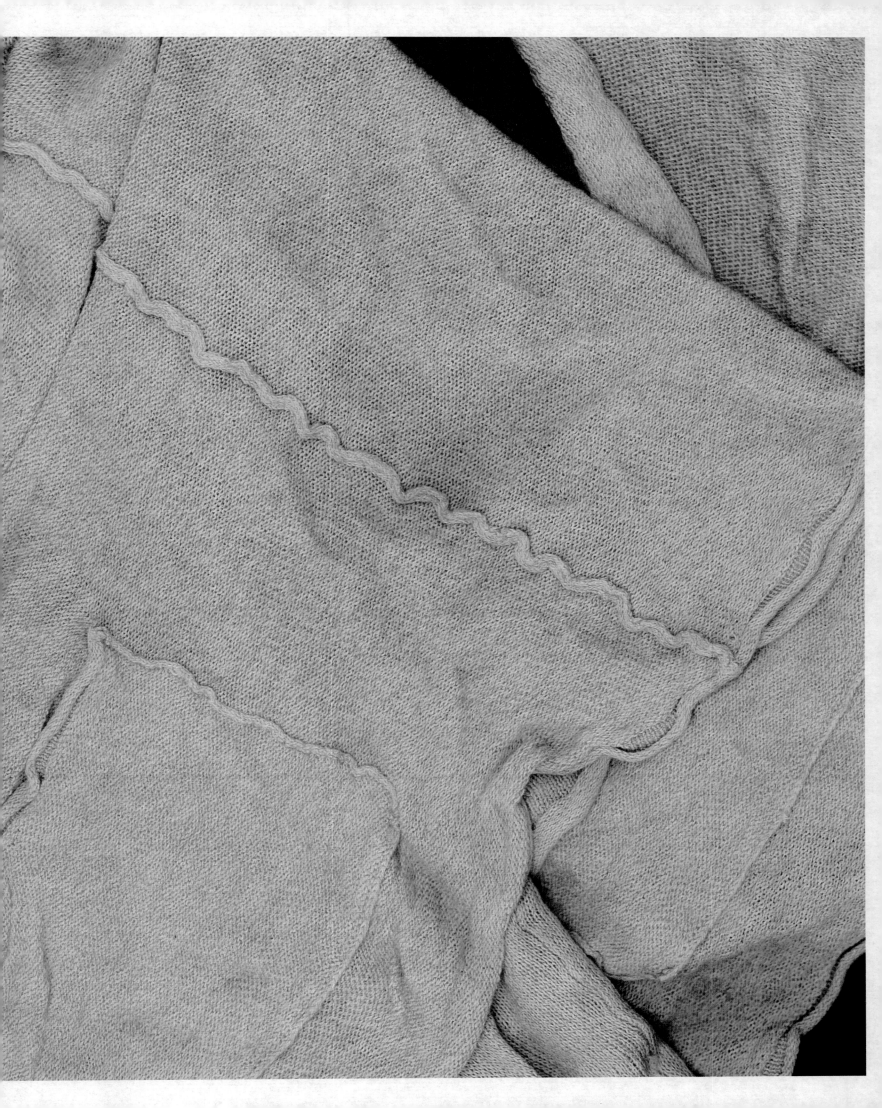

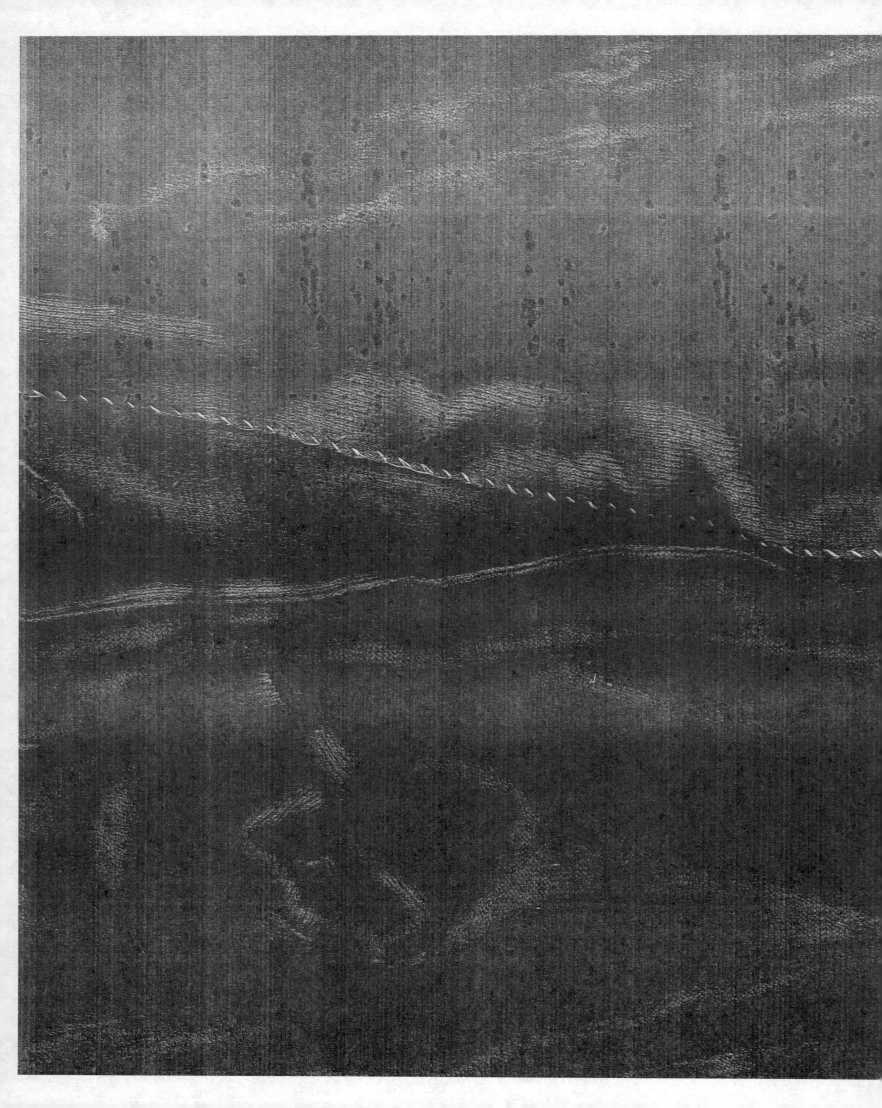

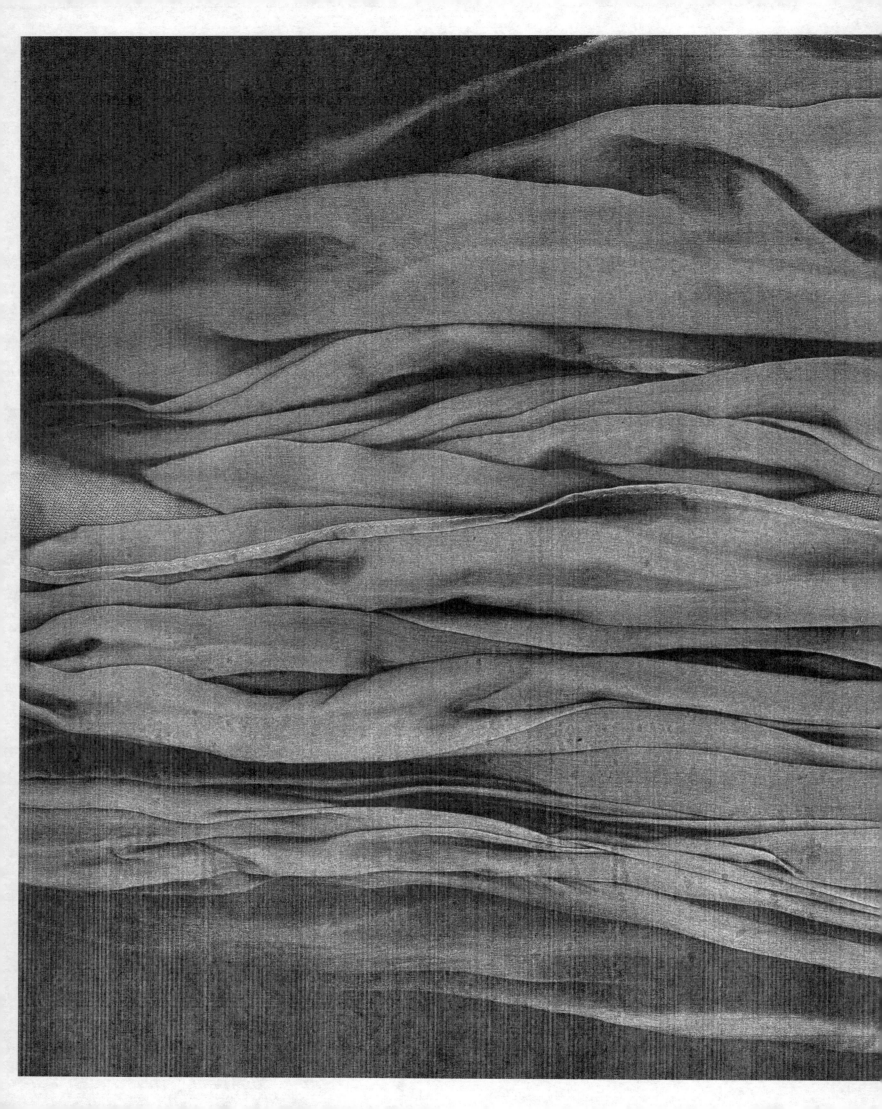

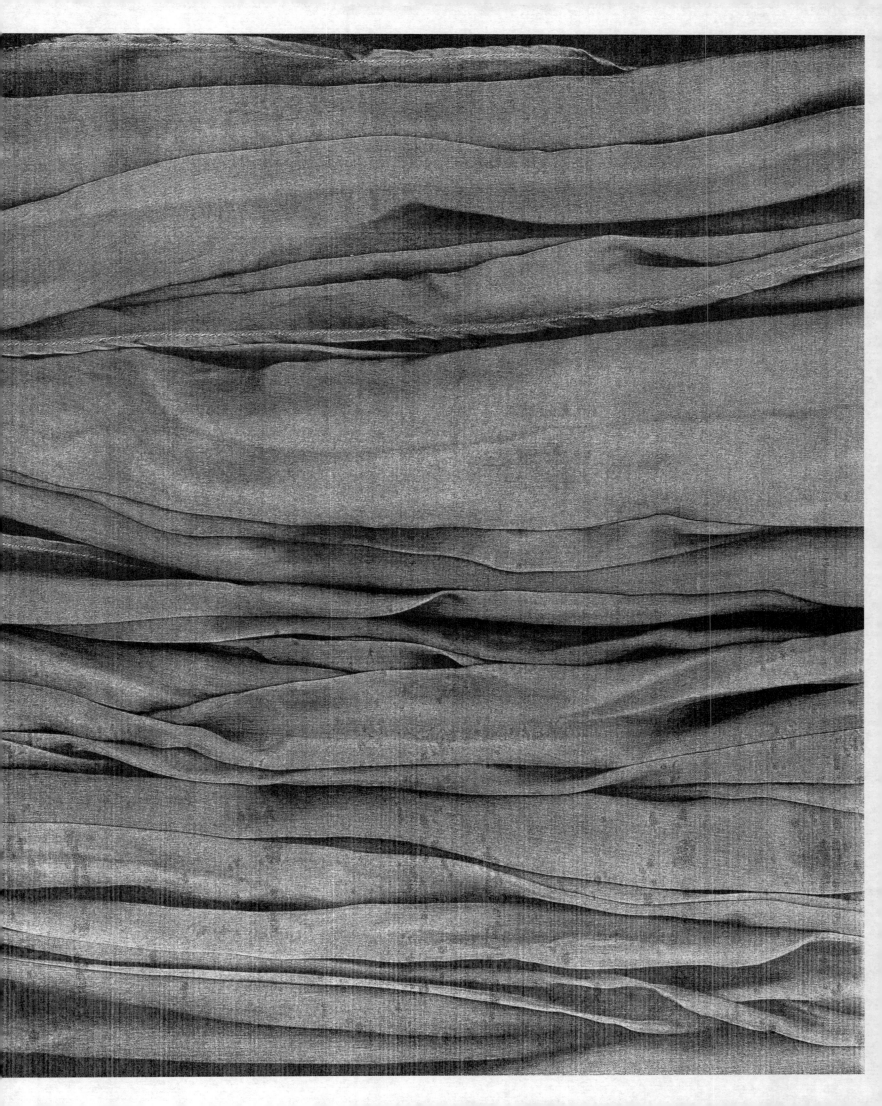

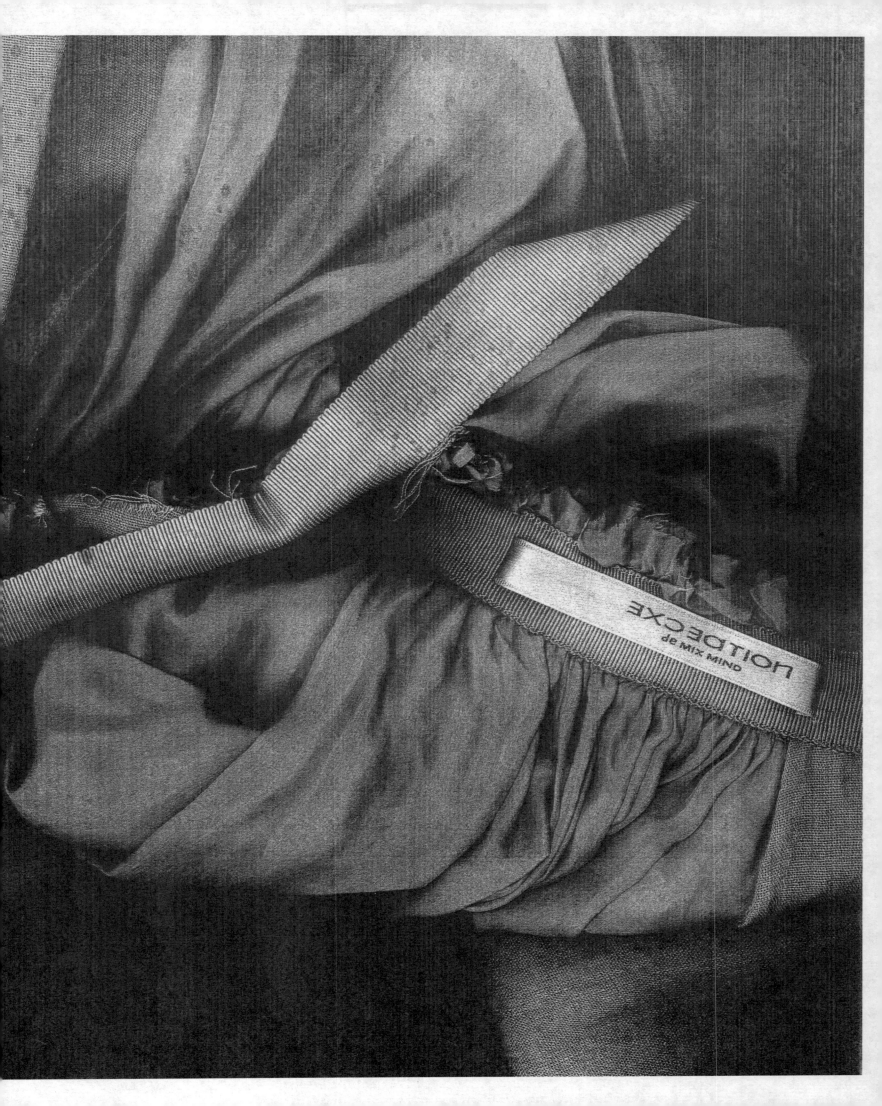

EXCEPTION
de MIX MIND

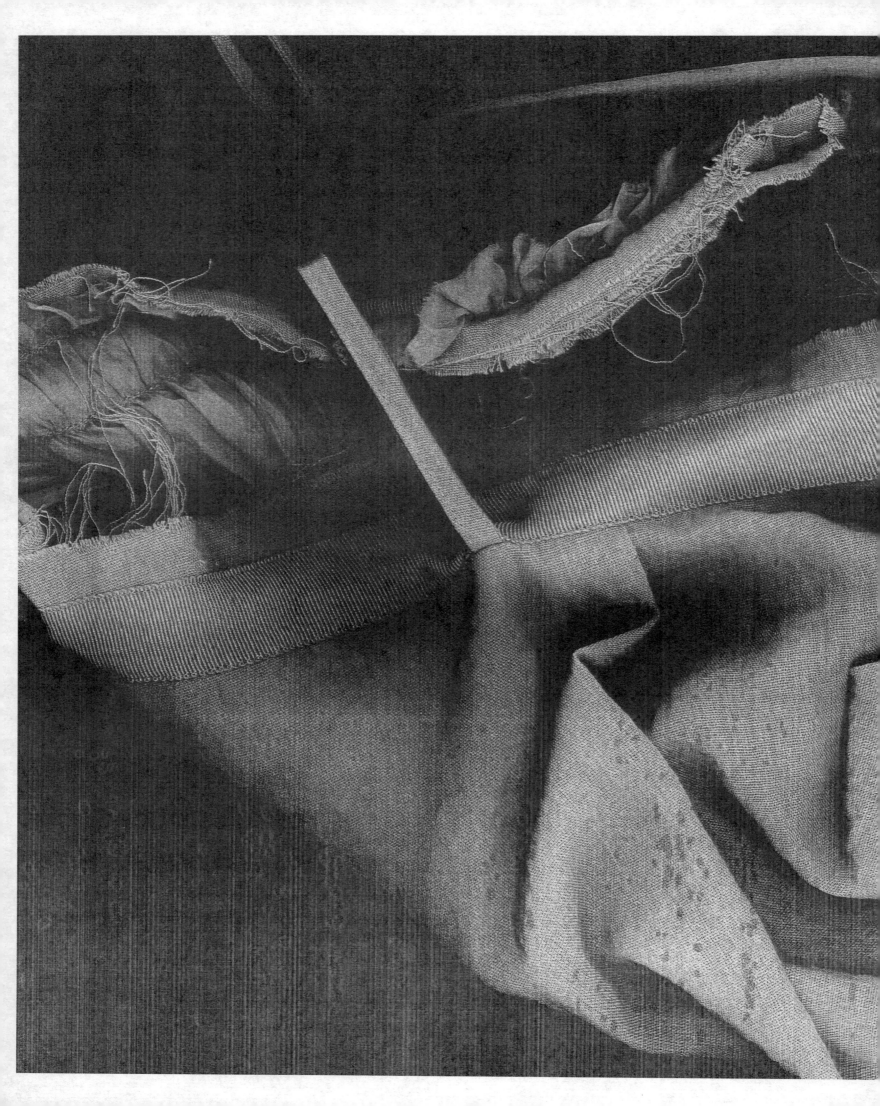

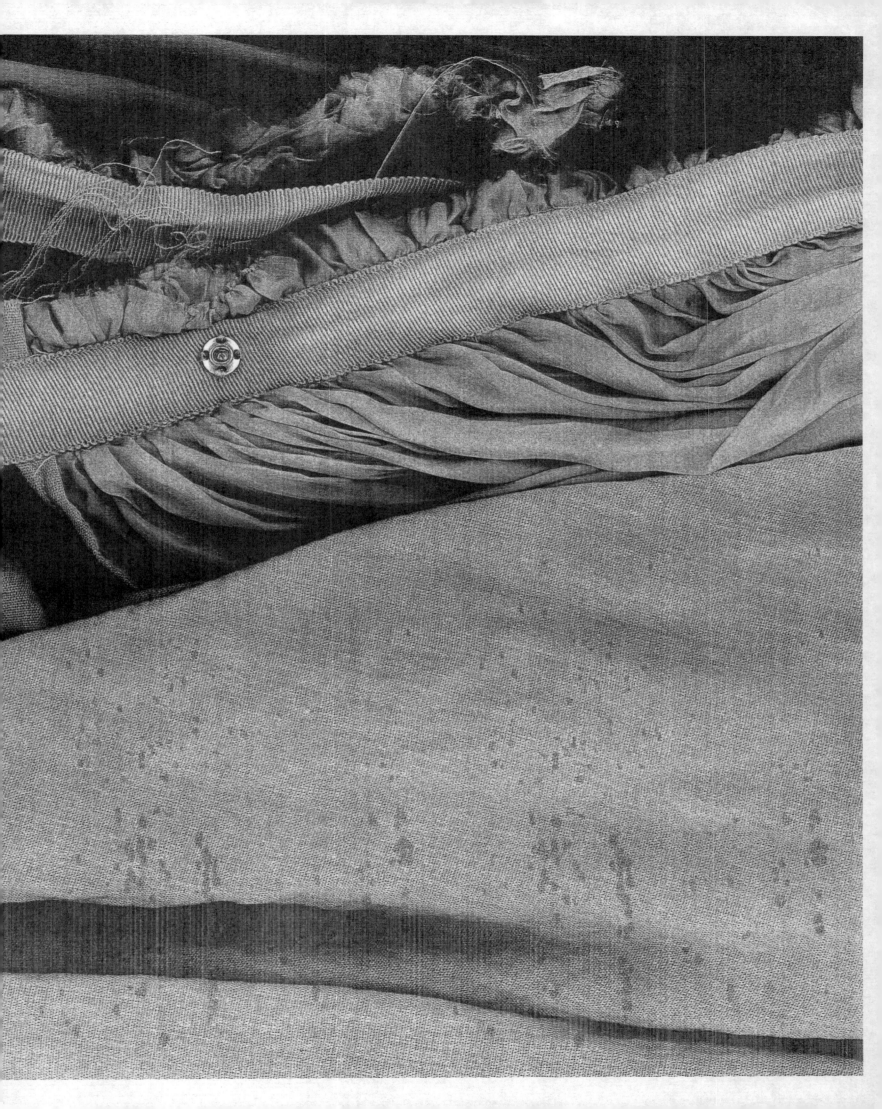

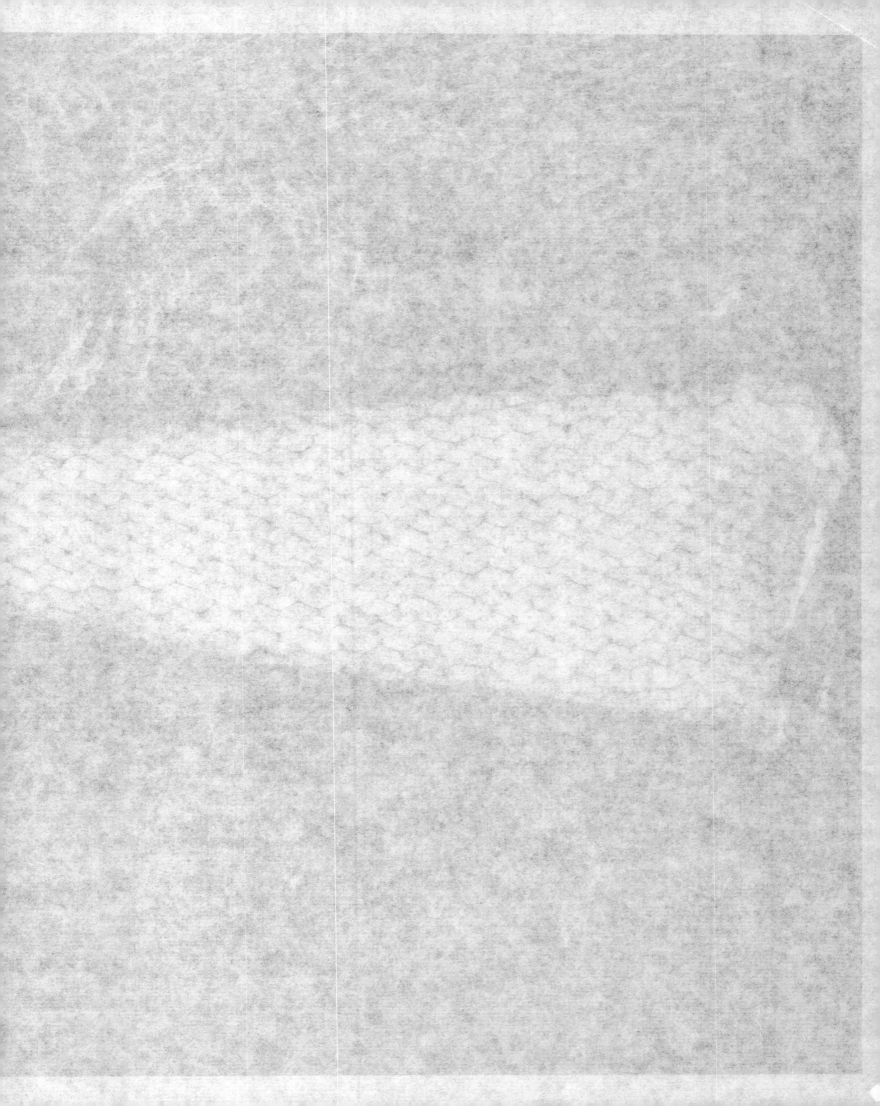

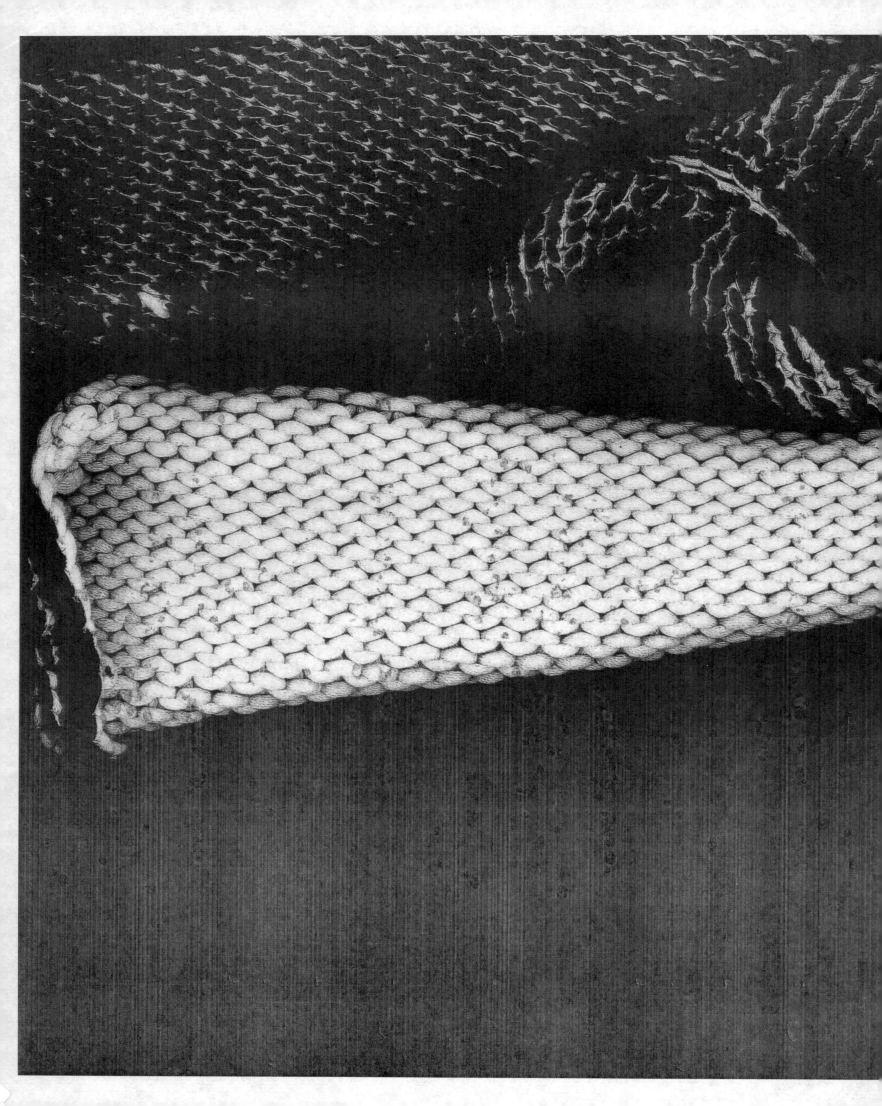

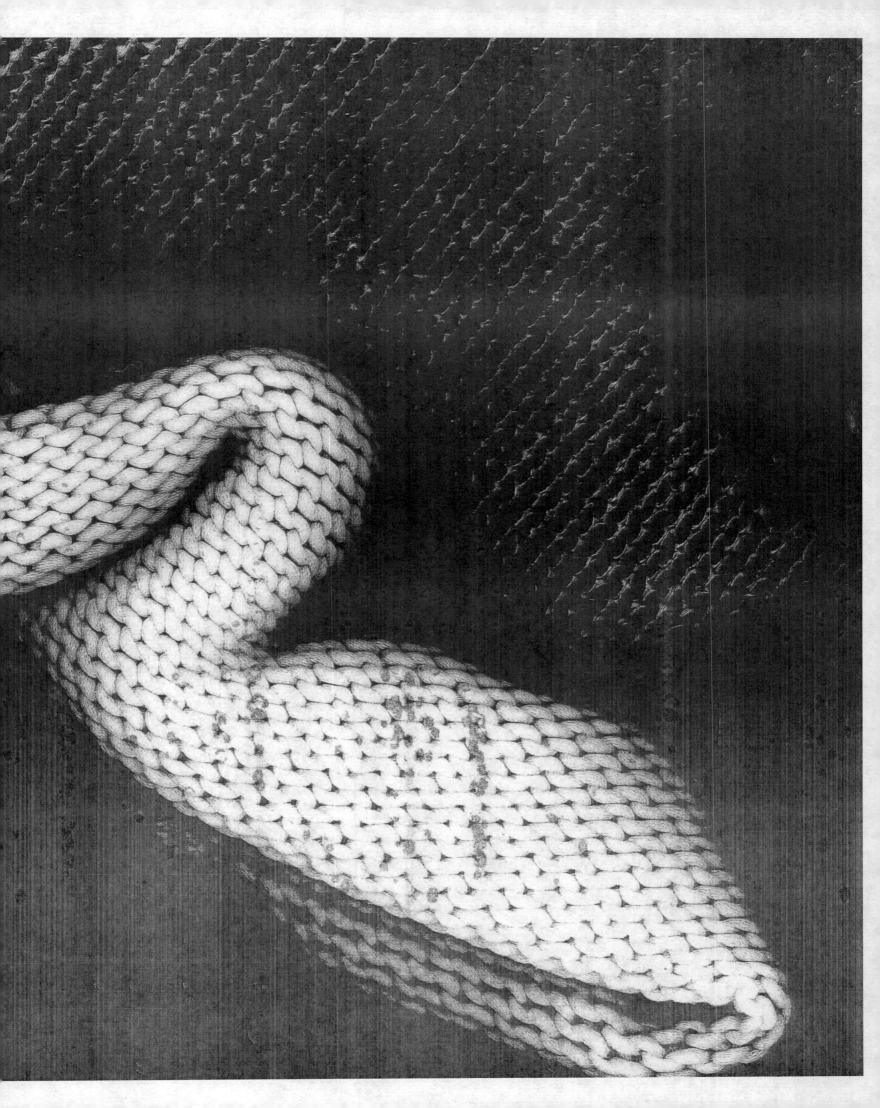

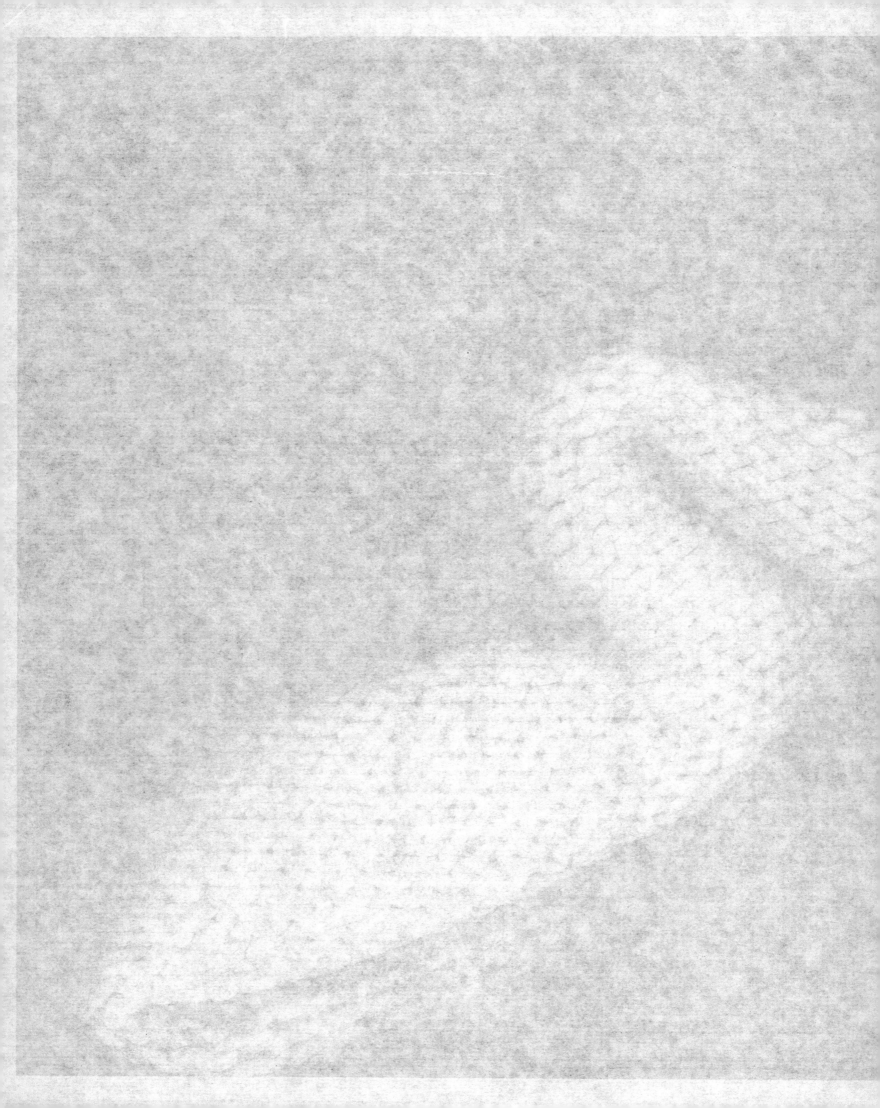

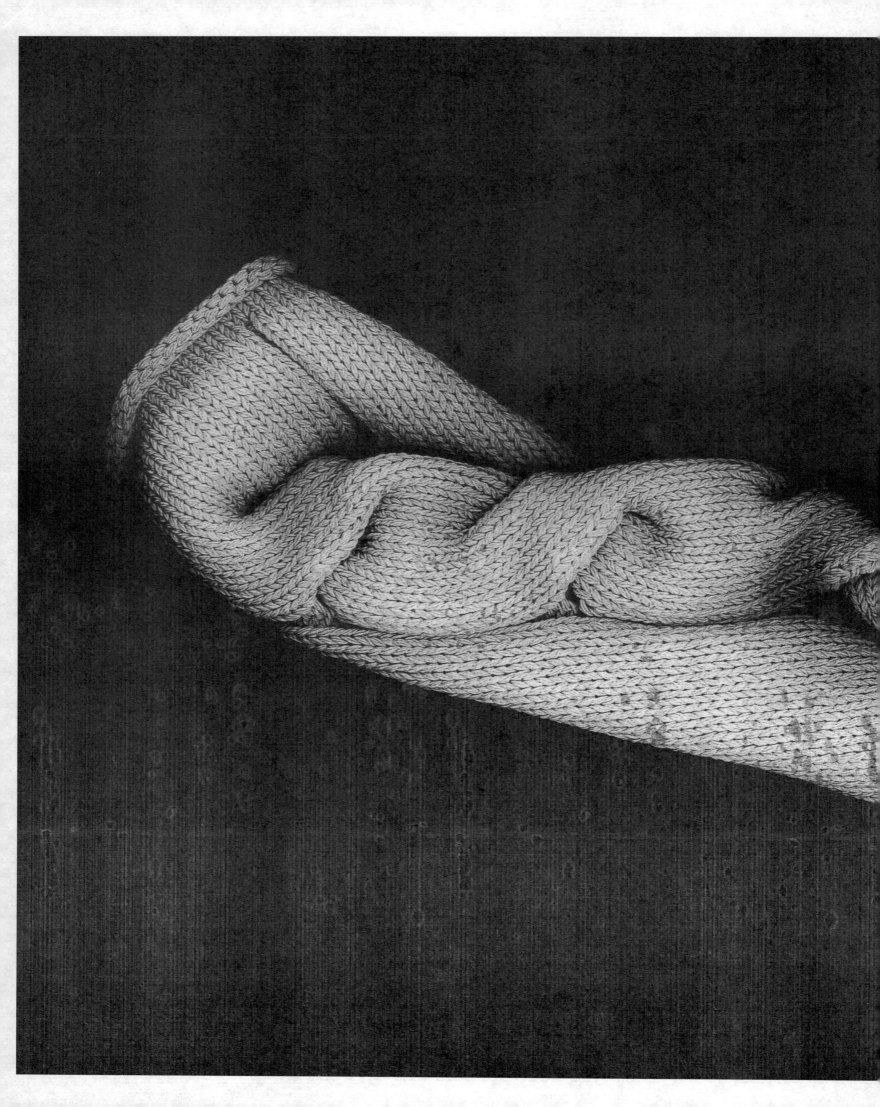

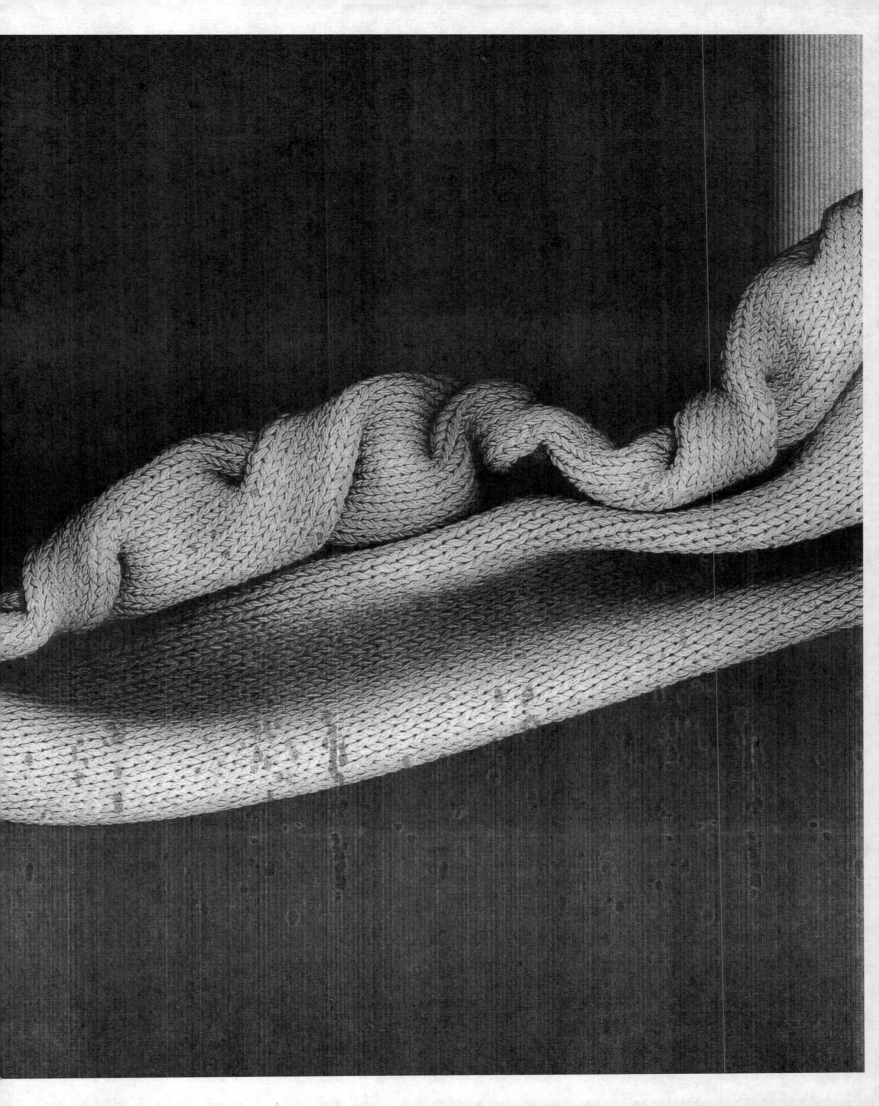

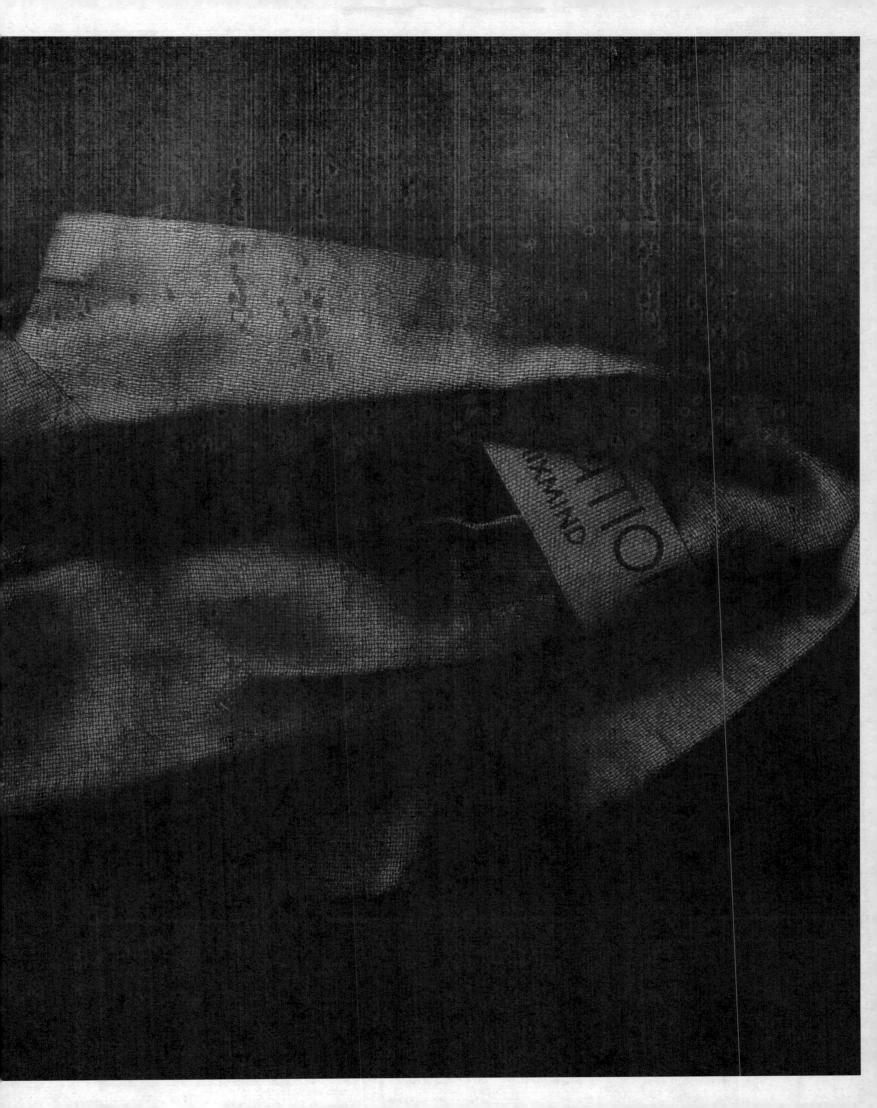

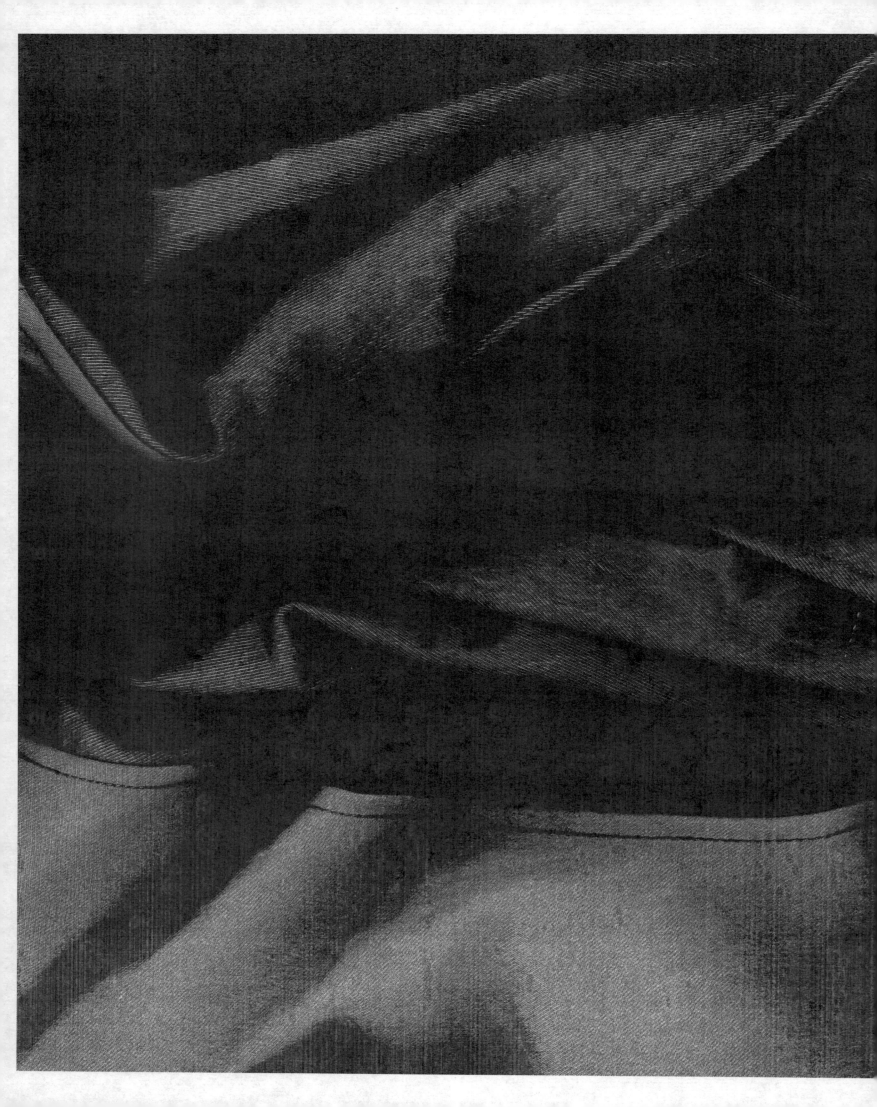

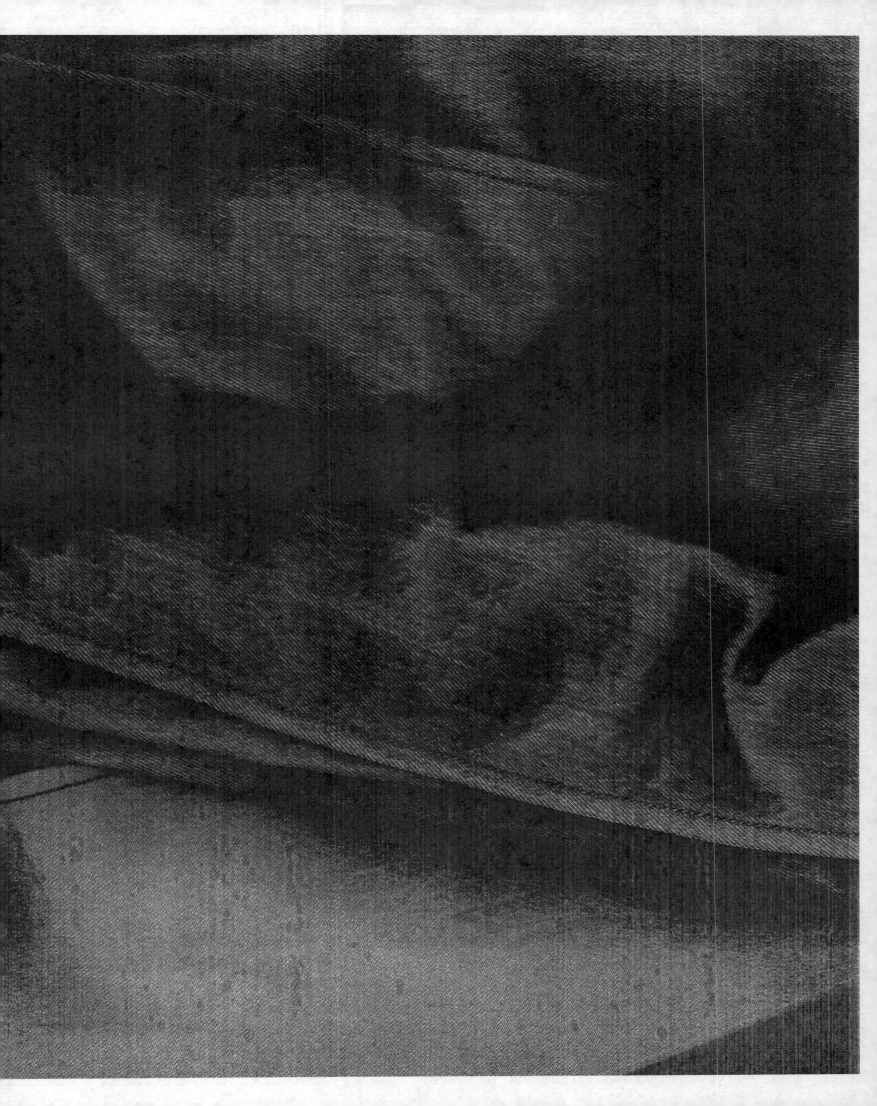

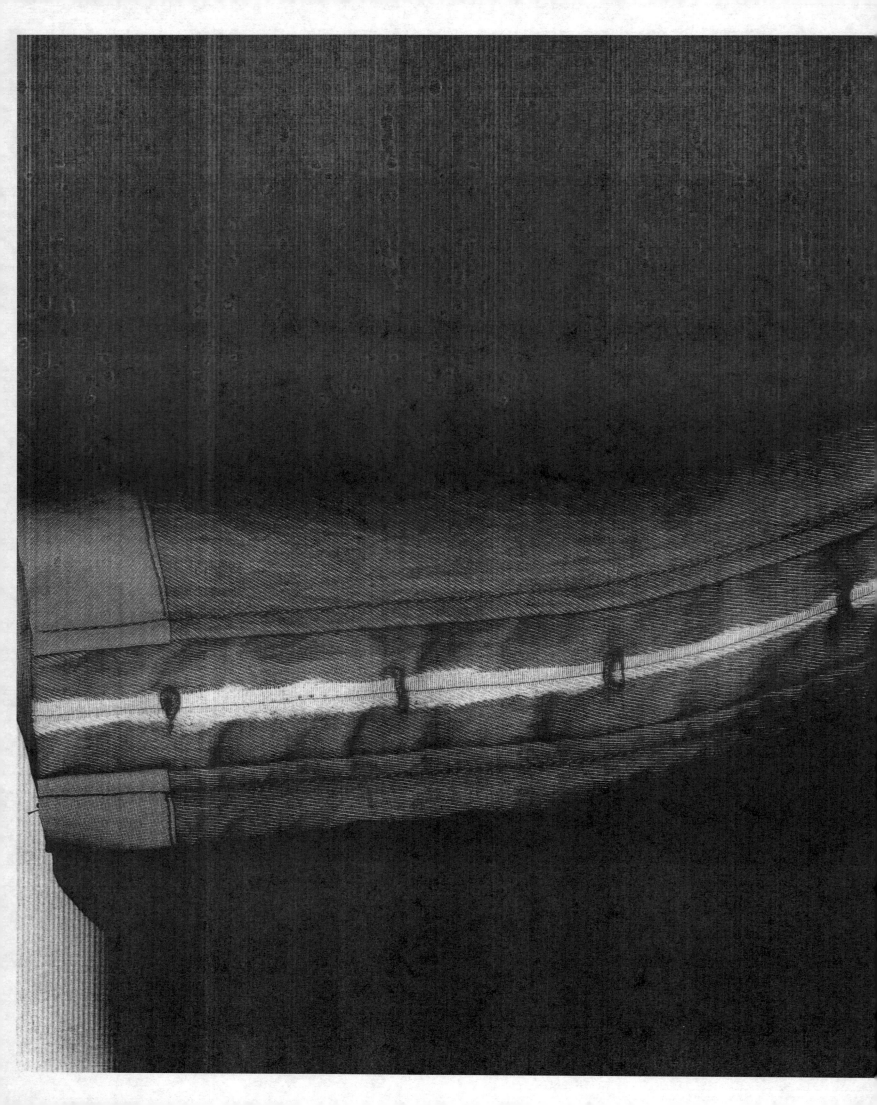

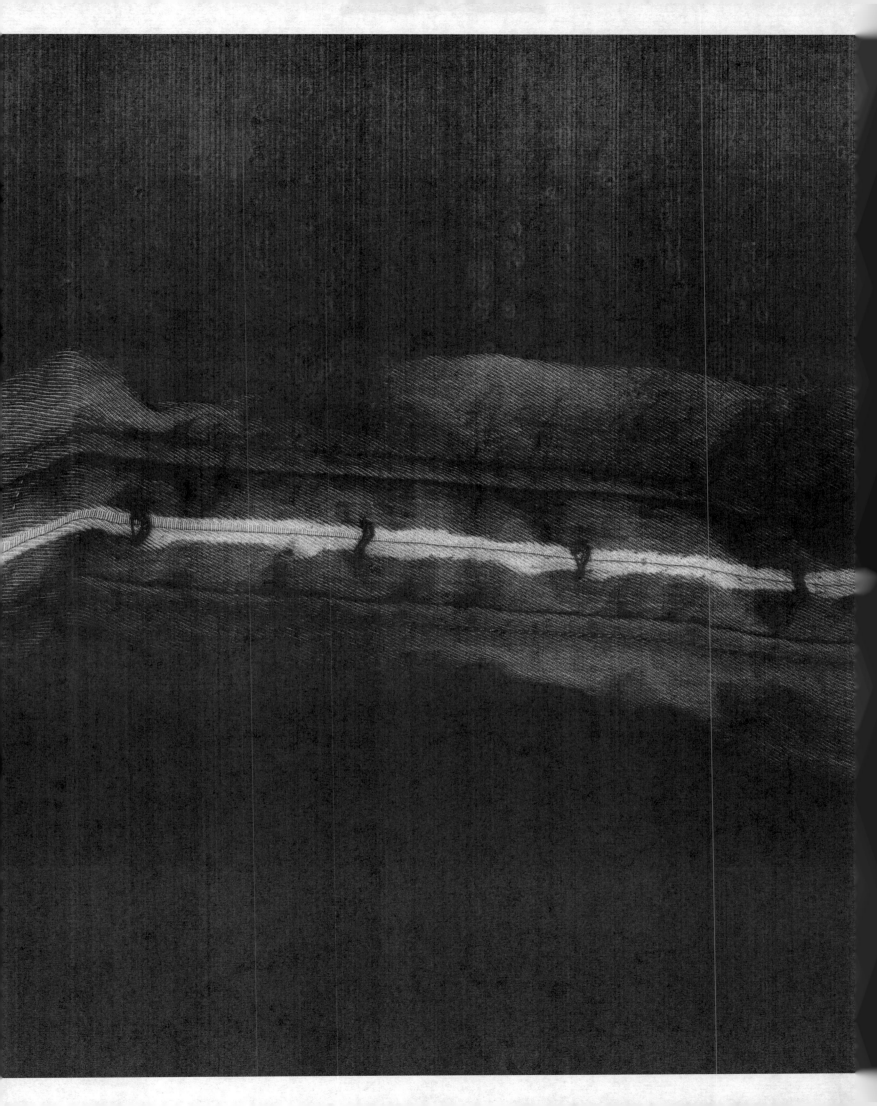

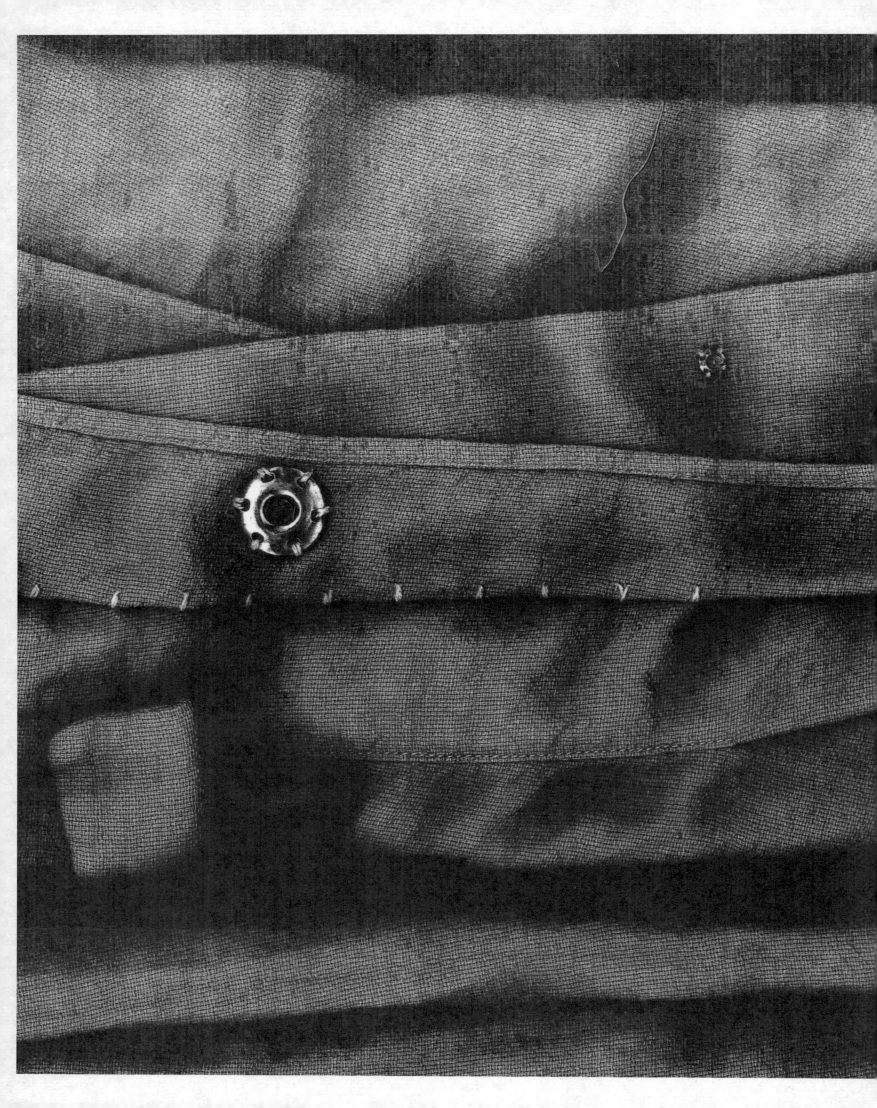

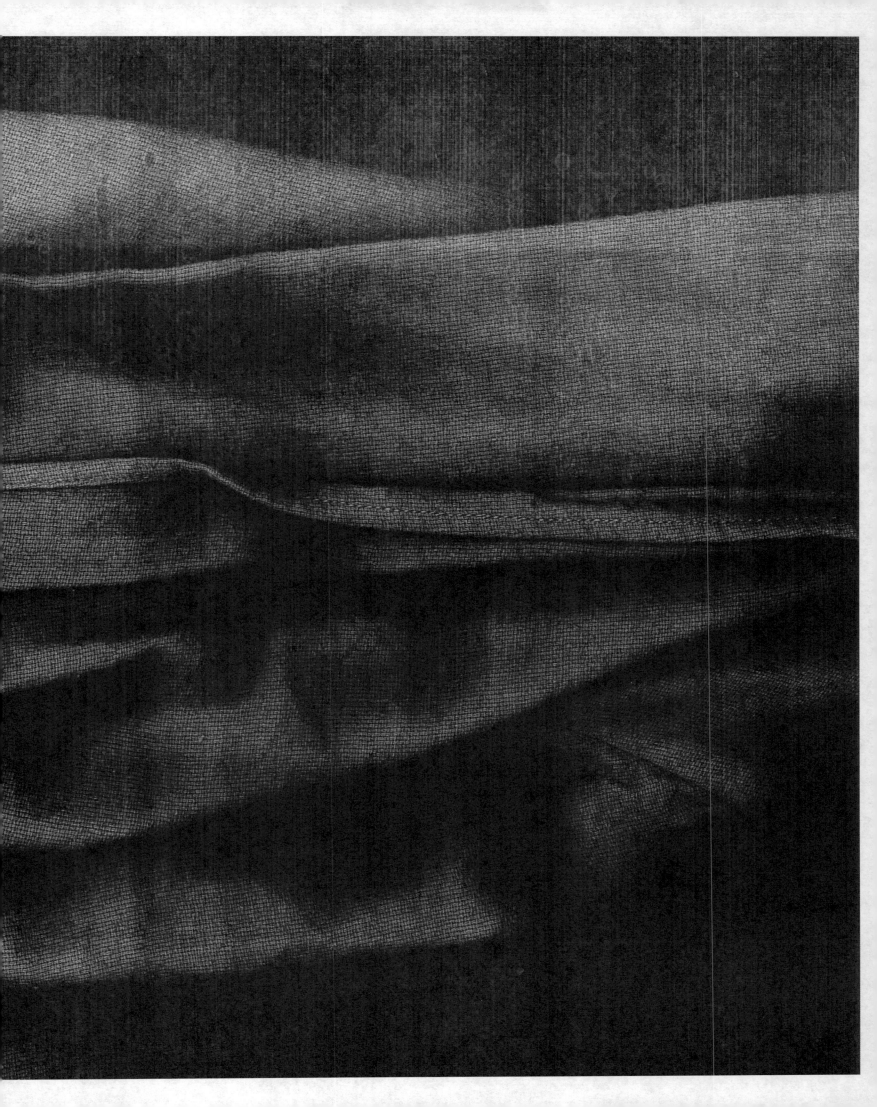

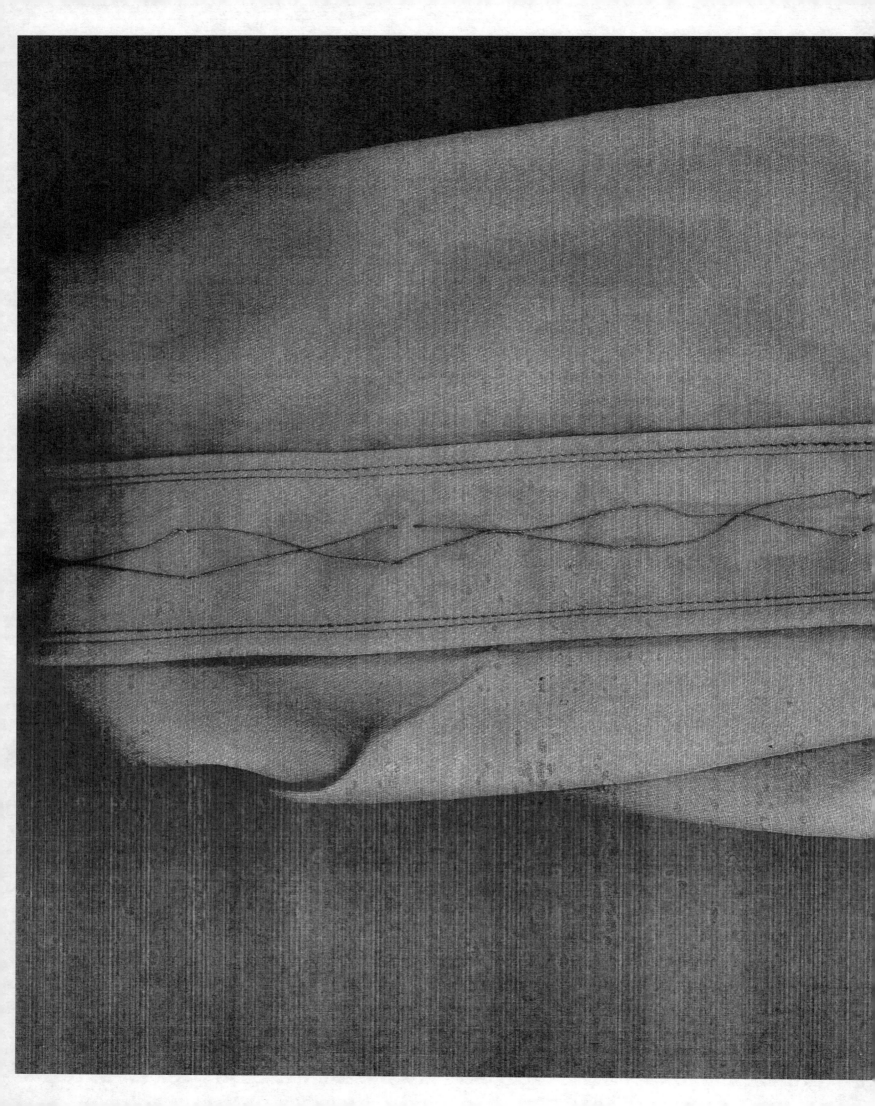

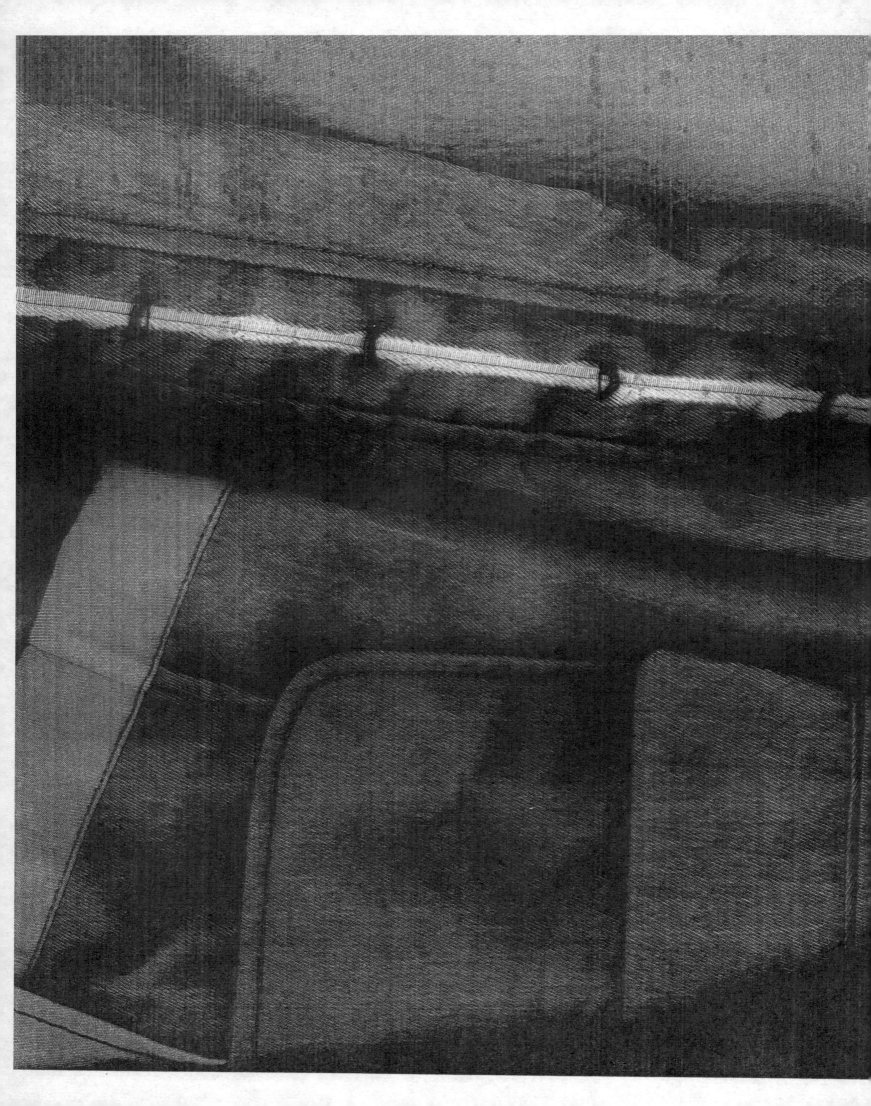

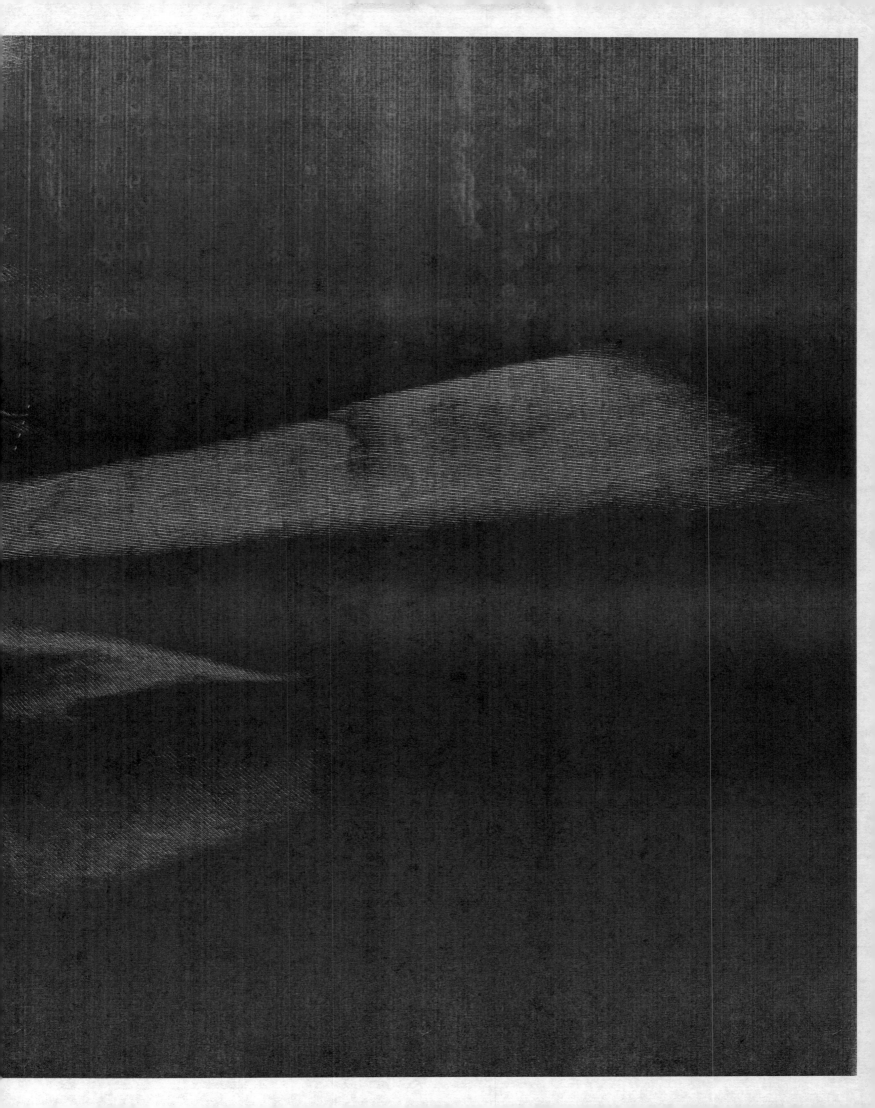

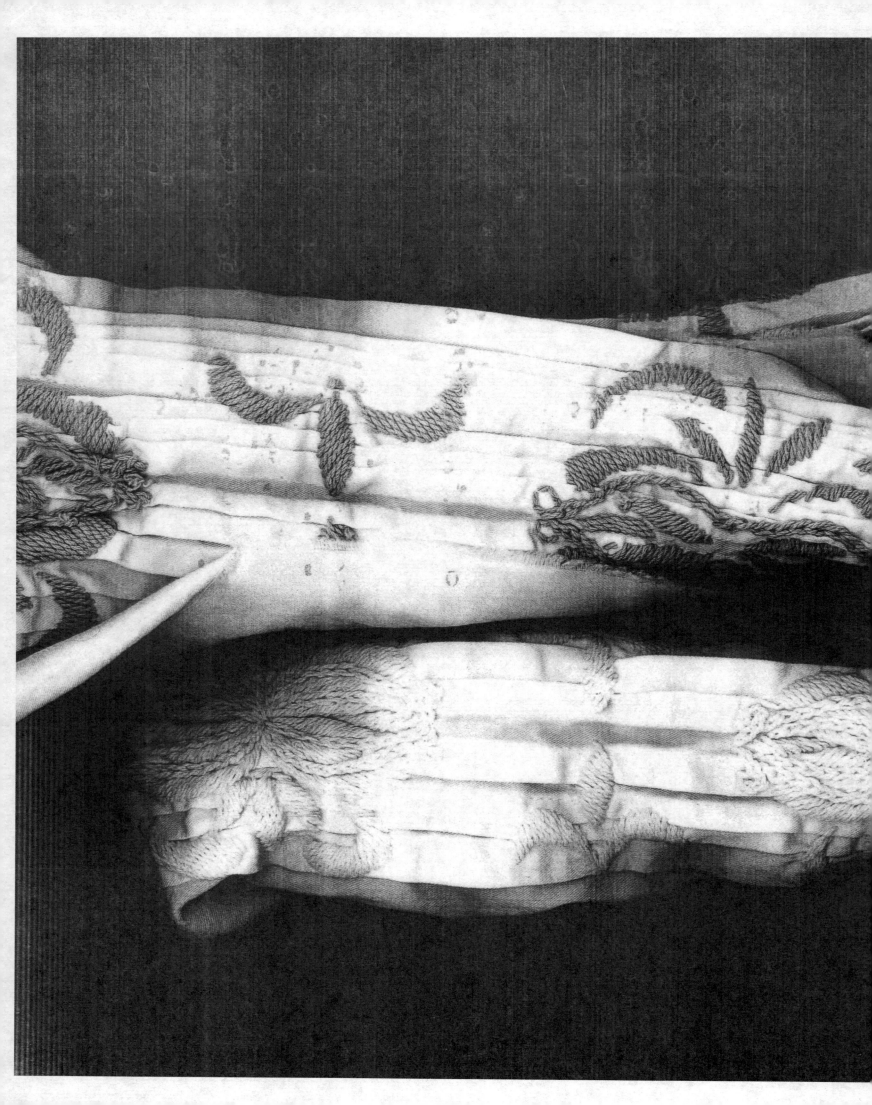

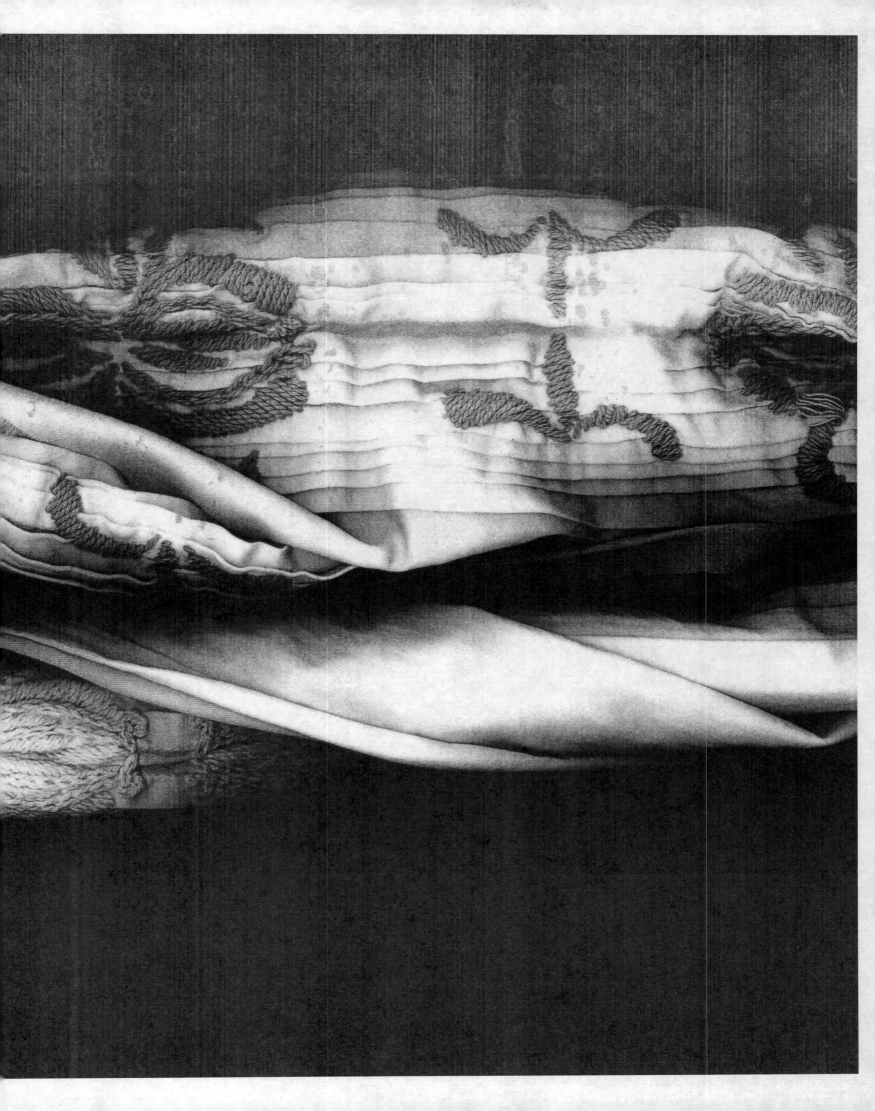

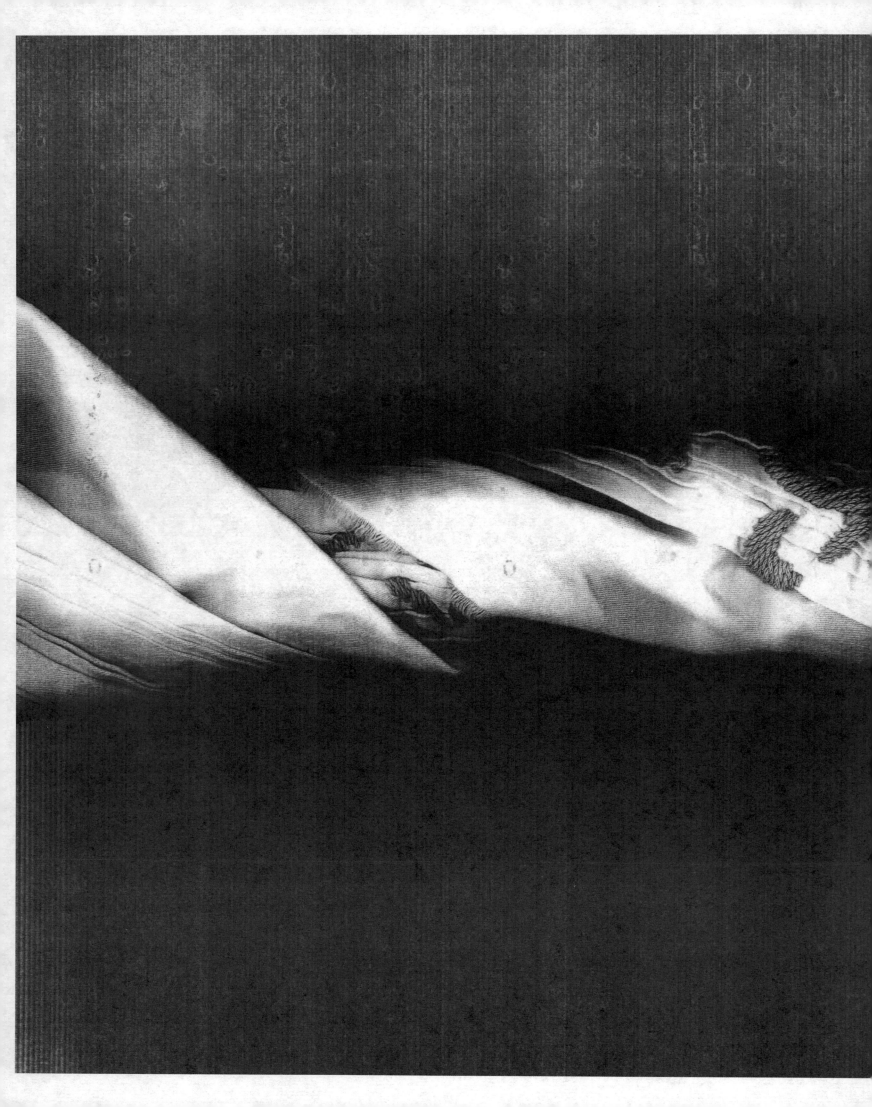

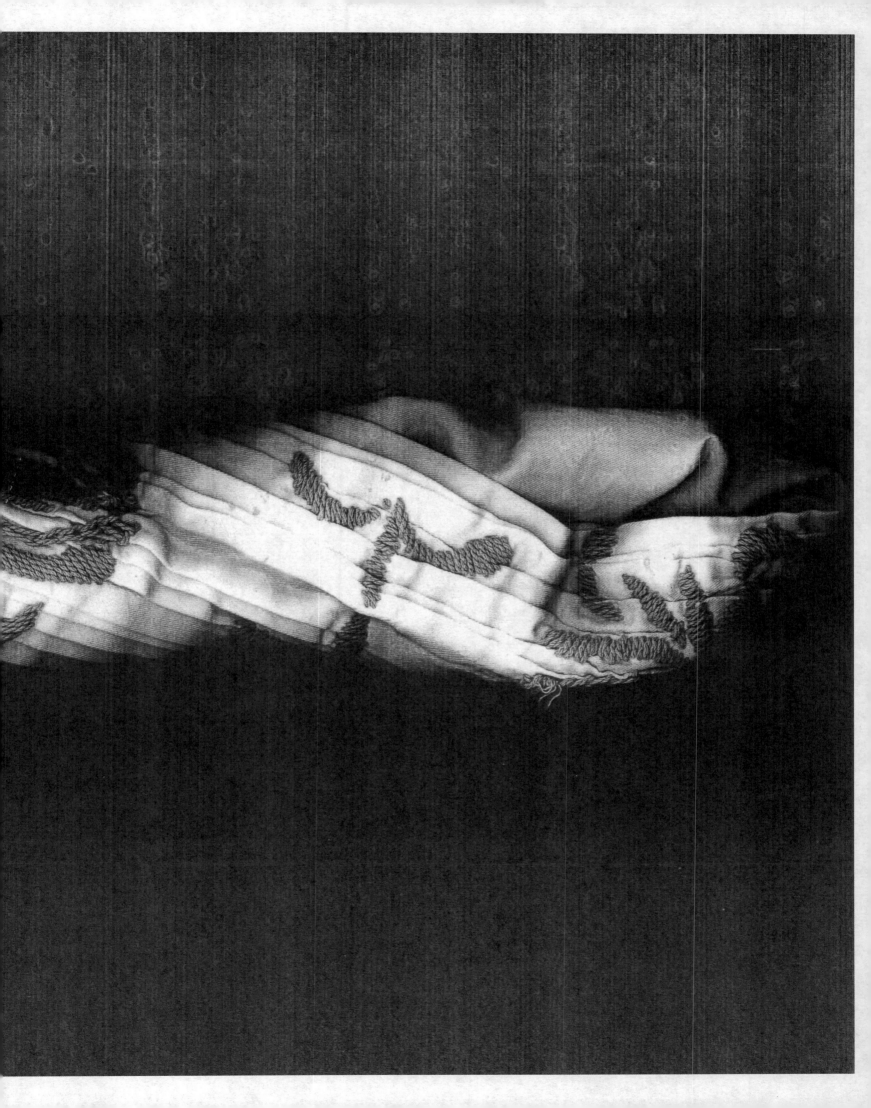

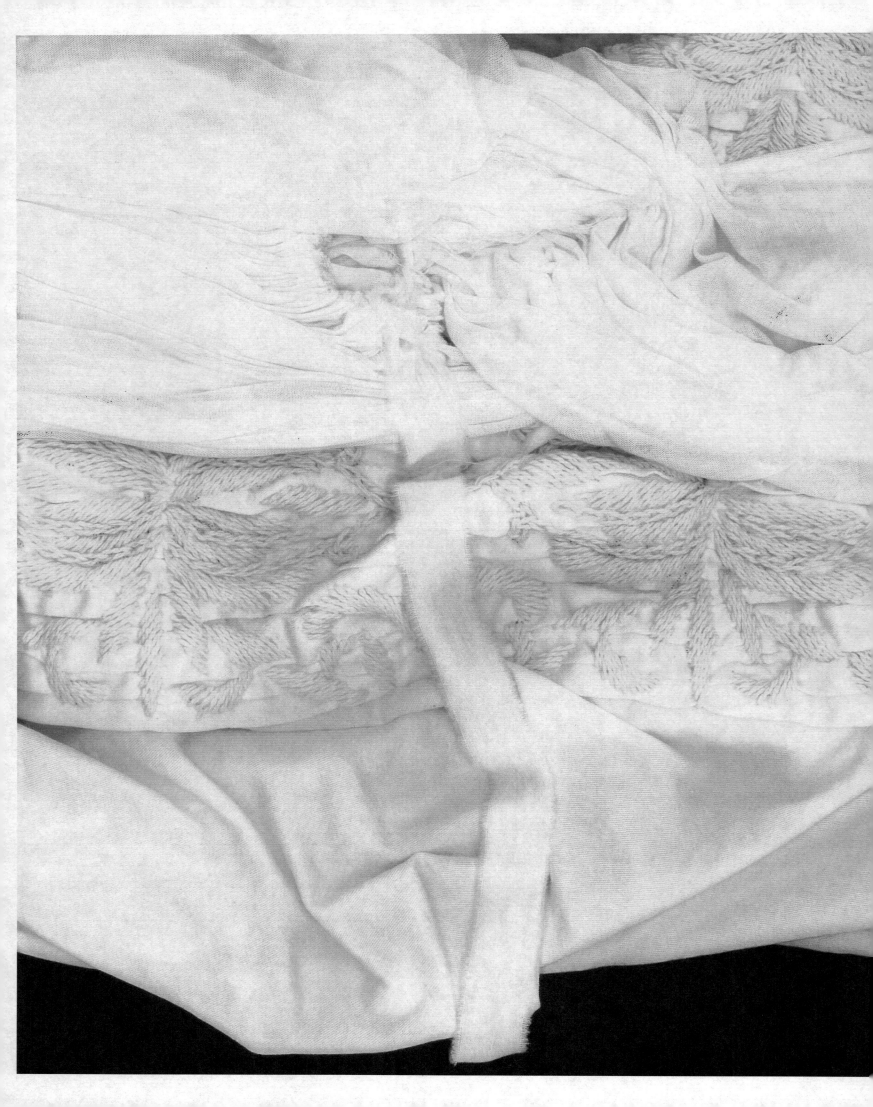

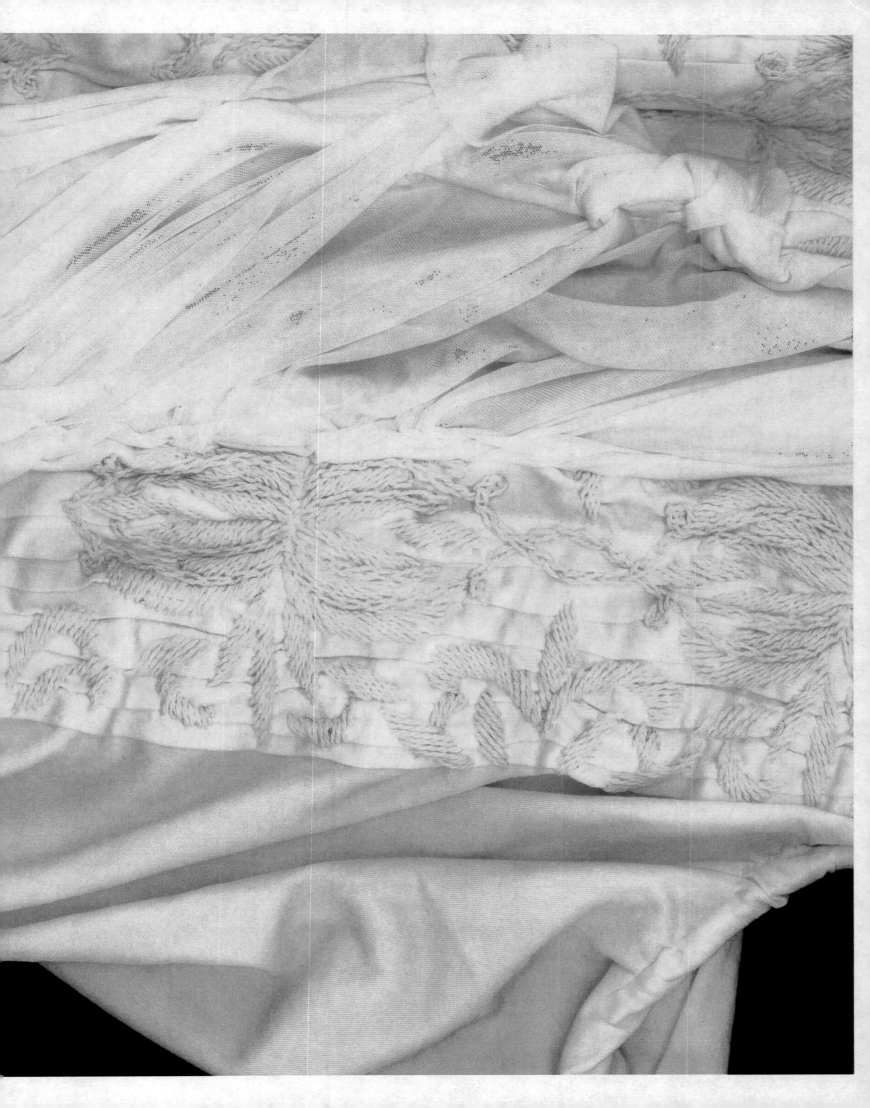

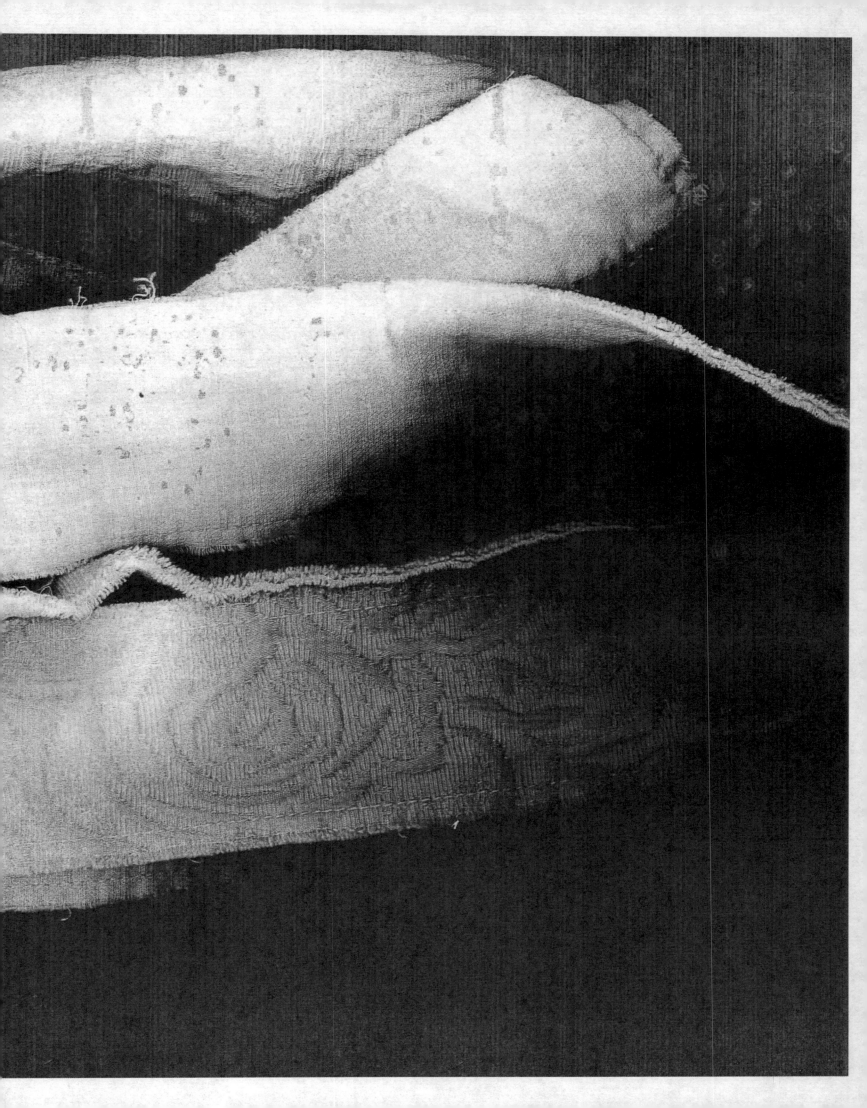

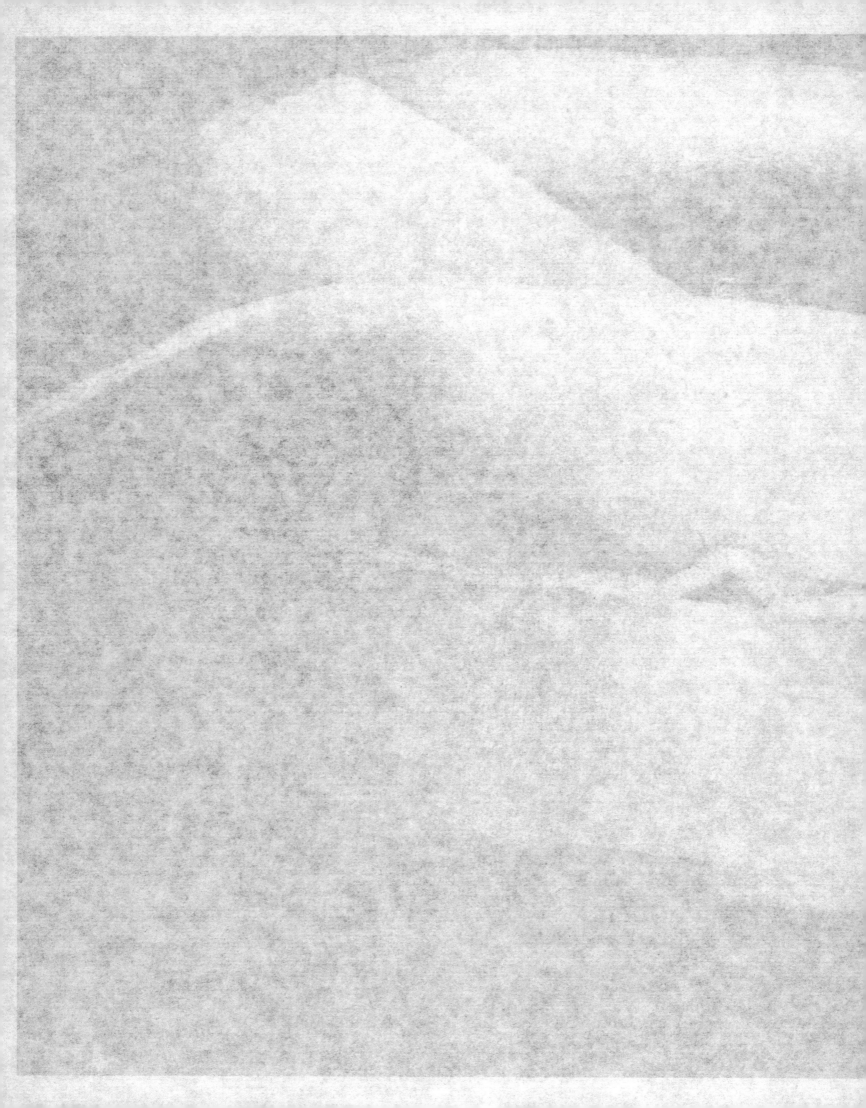

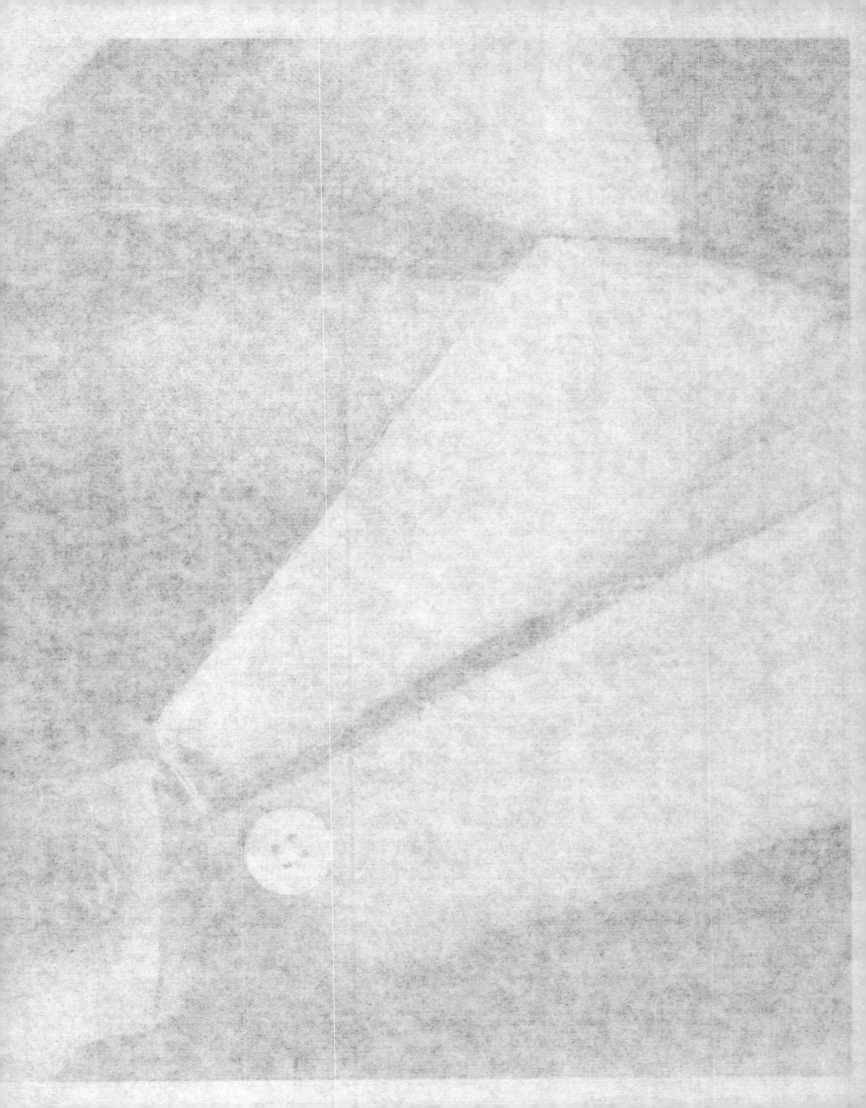

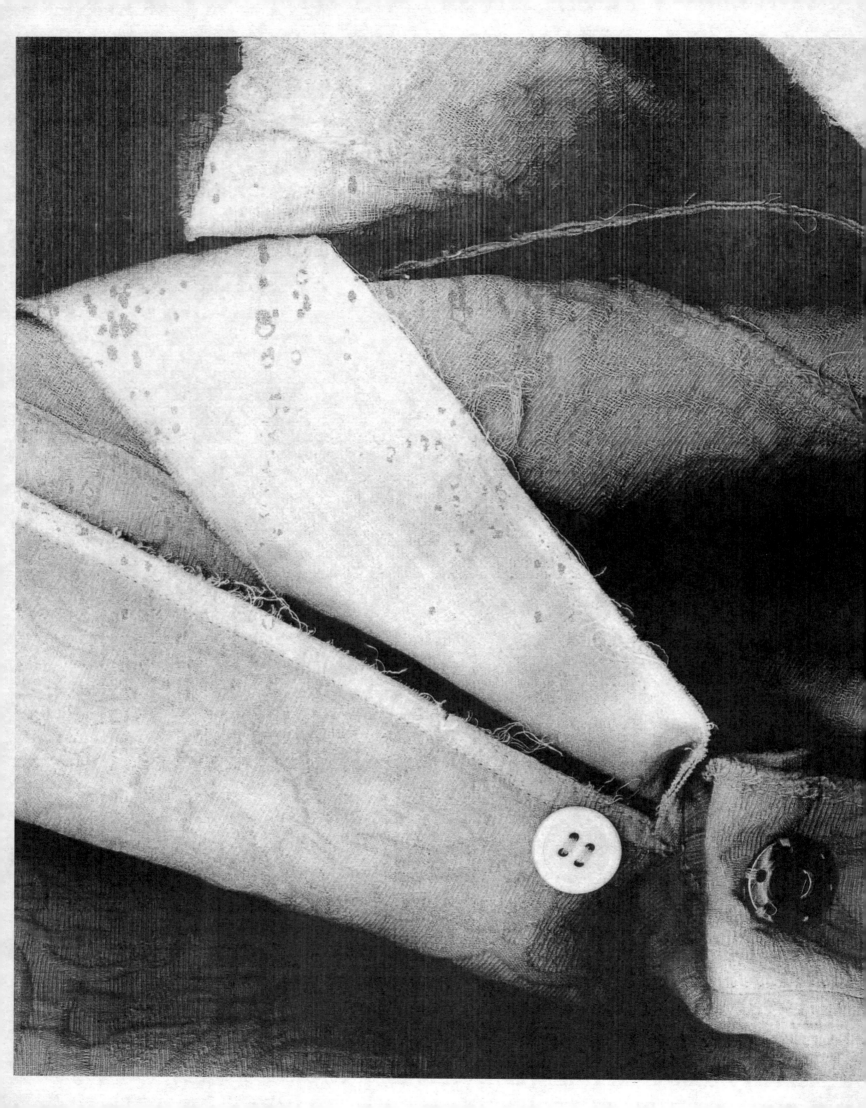

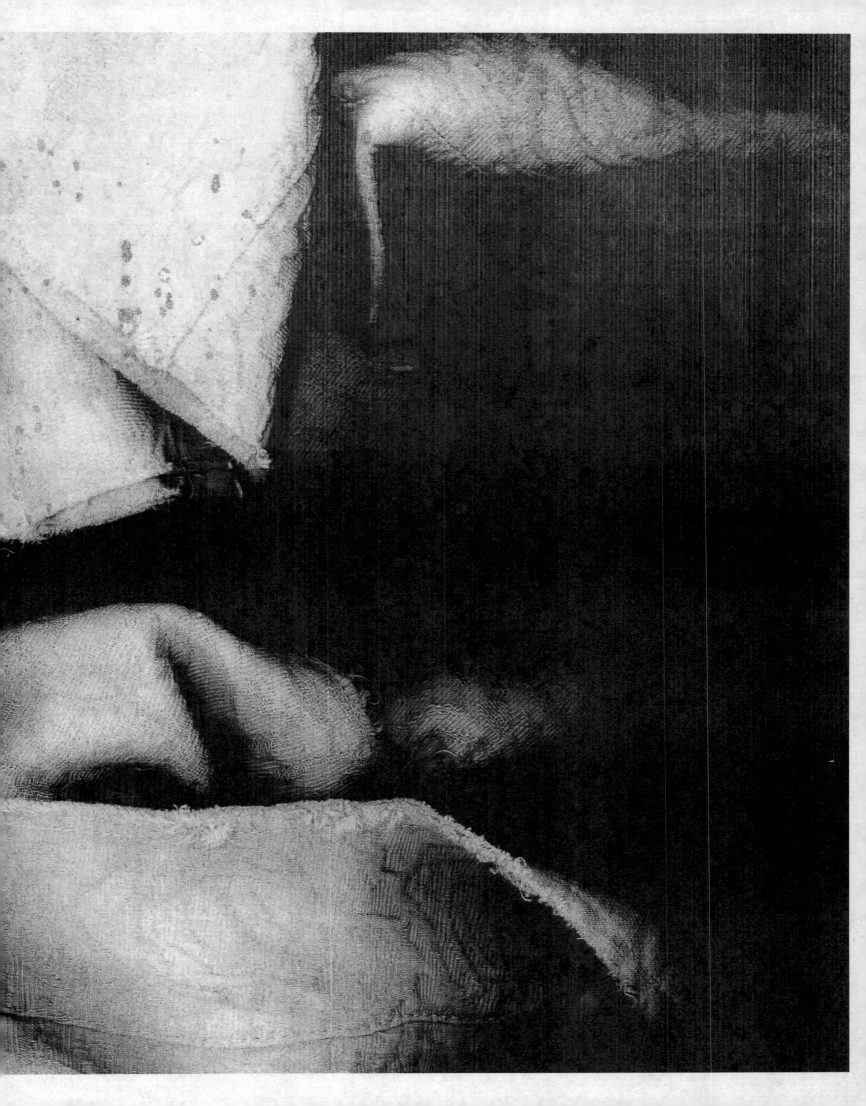

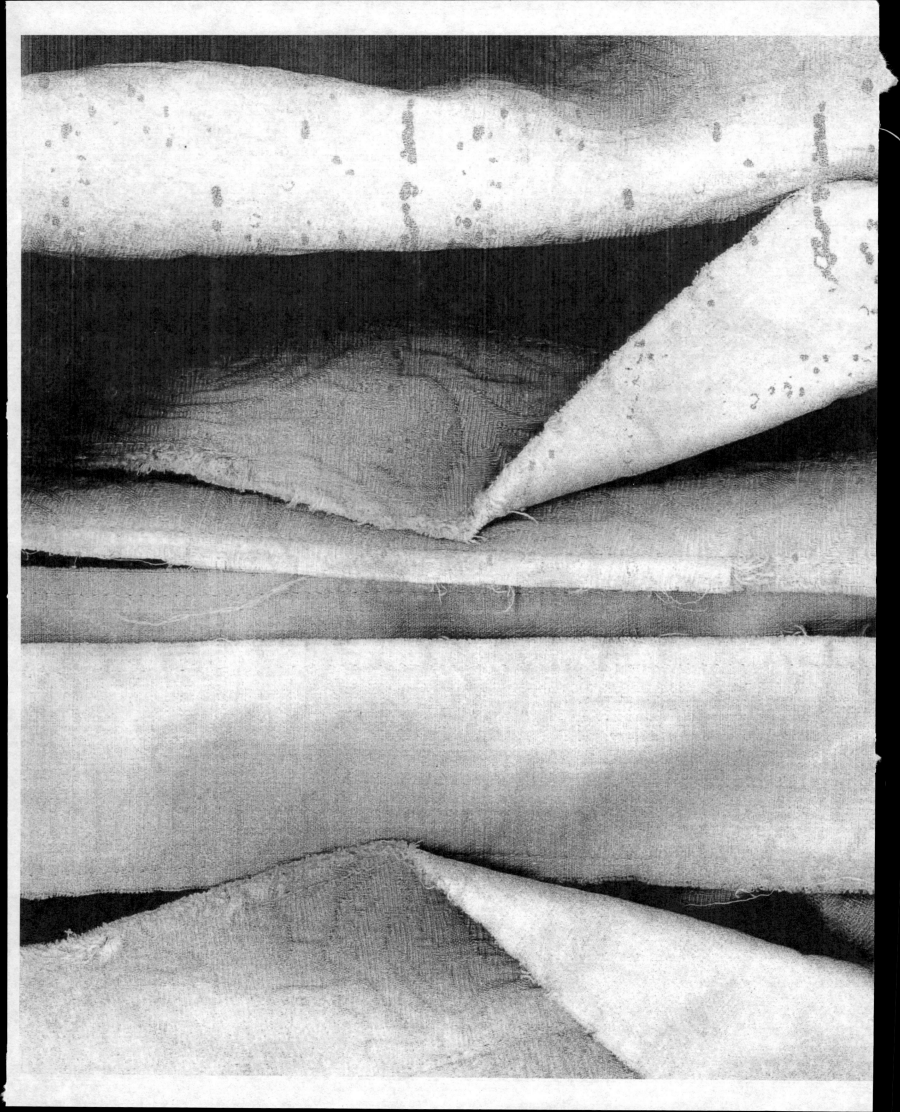

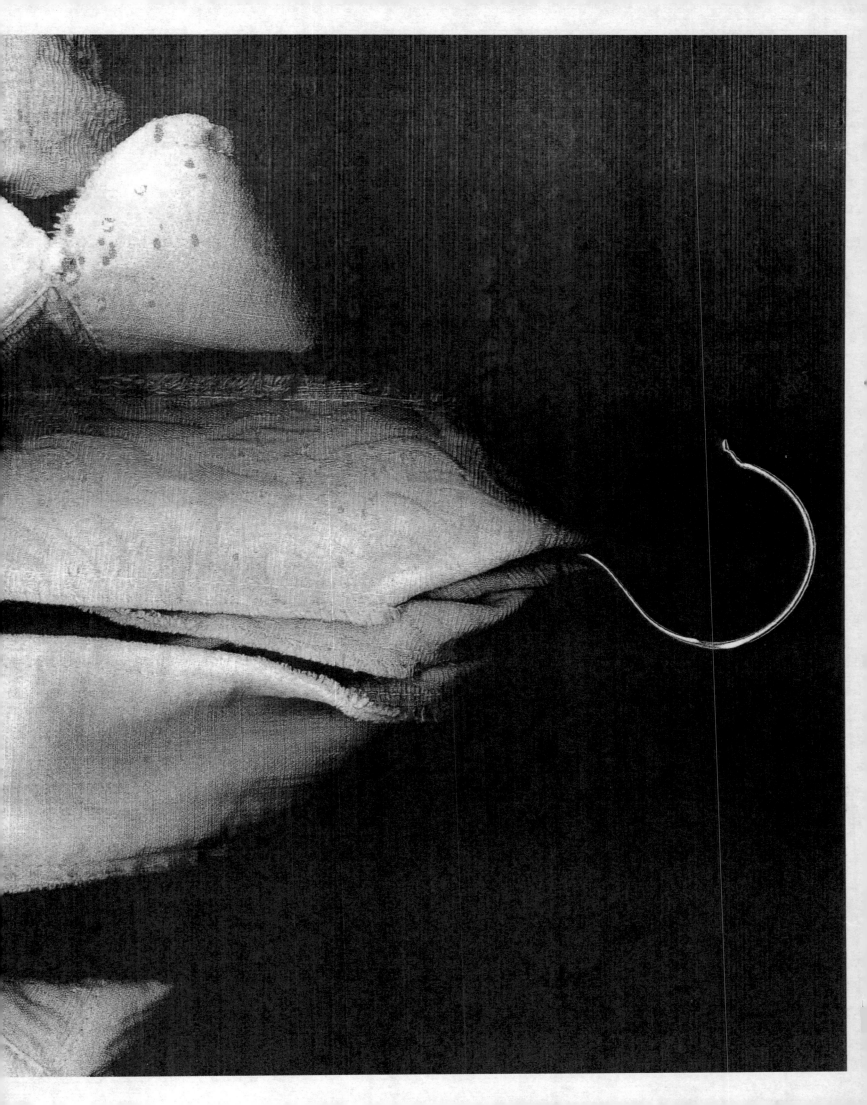

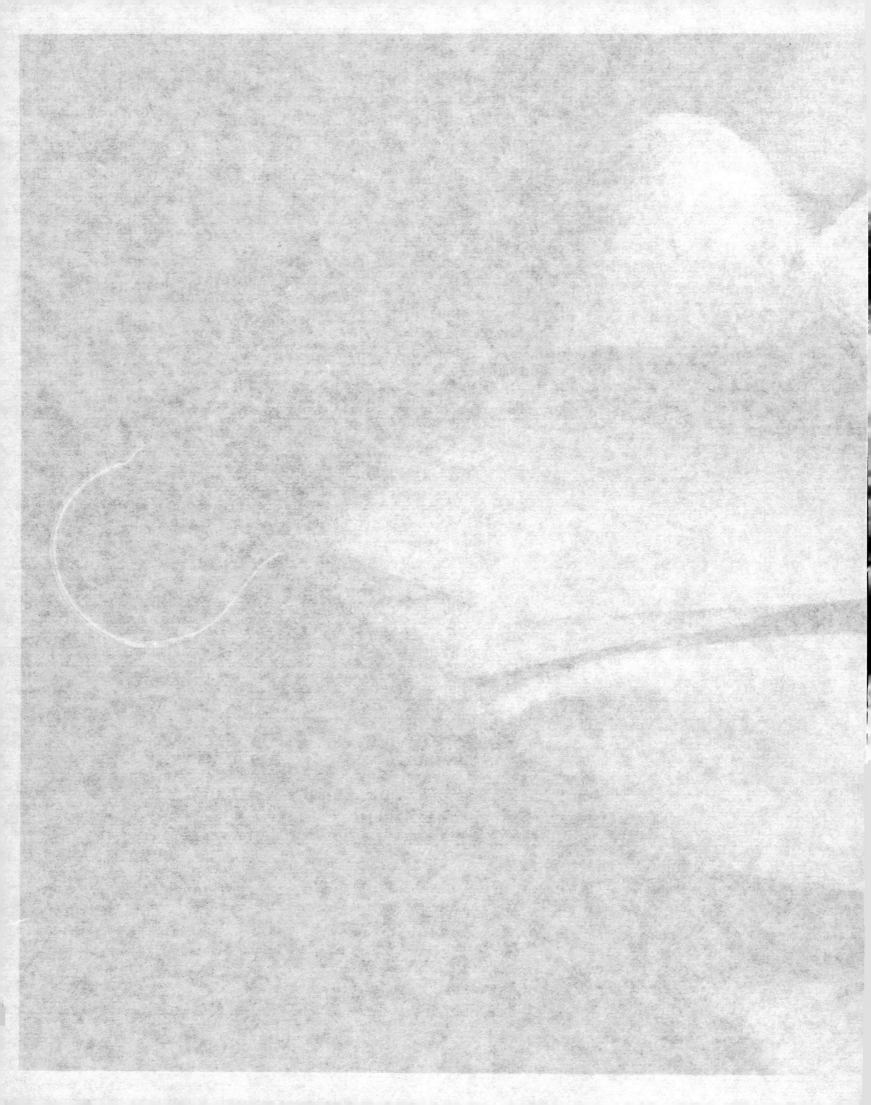

EXCEPTION
de MIXMIND

网址: http://www.mixmind.com

北京发布会工作人员名单 /

创意策划 / 马可 / **服装设计** / 陈海川 / **摄影** / 马可 / **书刊/平面设计** / 又一山人 /

组织统筹 / 毛继鸿 / 陈海川 / 张海儿 / 又一山人 / 舒雷 / 又一山人

工作人员 / 方宏桂 / 石志洁 / 叶萌萌 / 刘芸 / 刘静 / 刘晓溪 / 刘旭东 / 刘爱红 / 宁雅芳 / 吴中署 / 沈子鸢 / 林德照 / 李卫 / 赵雪琴 / 赵晓暖 / 赵红 / 罗华 / 钟云峰 / 唐秀兰 / 陆阳 /
陈军 / 黄尚 / 黄伶俐 / 邹鹏 / 覃海霞 / 曾庆海 / 程时国 / 张凤英 / 张方涛 / 张琳琳 / 张家新 / 梁嘉艳 / 舒韶灵 / 魏桂青 /

Beijing Fashion Show Credit /

Creative Director / Ma Ke / **Executive Director** / Chen Haichuan / Mao Jihong / **Fashion Designer** / Ma Ke /

Photographer / Zhang Hai'er / Anothermountainman / Shu Lei / **Graphic Designer** / Anothermountainman /

Excutive Member / Casper Leung / Chen Jun / Cheng Shiguo / Deng Li / Fang Honggui / Huang Lingli / Huang Shang / Li Wei / Lin Dezhao / Liu Aihong / Liu Hongsheng / Liu Jing /
Liu Yun / Liu Xiaoxi / Liu Xudong / Lu Yang / Luo Hua / Ning Yafang / Qin Haixia / Shen Ziying / Shi Zhijie / Shu Lei / Tang Xiulan / Wei Guiqing / Wu Zhongshu / Xie Shaoling /
Ye Mengmeng / Zeng Qinghai / Zhang Fangtao / Zhang Fengying / Zhang Jiaxin / Zhang Linlin / Zhao Hong / Zhao Xiaoyuan / Zhao Xueqin / Zhong Yunfeng / Zou Peng /